RECOVERING
LOST
TREASURE

FINDING CHRIST IN ANCIENT
MYTH, SYMBOL, AND RITUAL

RECOVERING LOST TREASURE

 FINDING CHRIST IN ANCIENT
MYTH, SYMBOL, AND RITUAL

Eric Odell-Hein

REDEMPTION
PRESS

Published by Redemption Press, PO Box 427, Enumclaw, WA 98022

Toll Free (844) 2REDEEM (273-3336)

Redemption Press is honored to present this title in partnership with the author. The views expressed or implied in this work are those of the author. Redemption Press provides our imprint seal representing design excellence, creative content, and high quality production.

All Scripture quotations, unless otherwise indicated, are taken from the New American Standard Bible® (NASB), Copyright © 1960, 1962, 1963, 1968, 1971, 1972, 1973, 1975, 1977, 1995 by The Lockman Foundation. Used by permission. www.Lockman.org

ISBN 13: 978-1-68314-402-1 (Paperback)
978-1-68314-418-2 (Hard Cover)
978-1-68314-403-8 (ePub)
978-1-68314-404-5 (Mobi)

Library of Congress Catalog Card Number:

Table of Contents

für Ephraim

Acknowledgments

MANY PEOPLE DESERVE THANKS AND acknowledgment for their contributions to this book and for their support of me during the past decade I have spent working on it. I am listing a few of them here, but there are many more that have played a role.

First, many thanks to Dr. Rick Walston. Rick was my personal mentor for much of my life as a student, and he has played a large role in my academic development. He is also a personal friend. You would be hard-pressed to find a better mentor for academic research anywhere.

My pastor, Rev. Ross Holtz, has been a constant encourager and a common discussion companion. He even tolerates my academic style to the point where he brought me on the ministry team as the Teaching Pastor. He's been both a mentor and a friend.

My friend Rev. Marcus Kelly has been a tremendous personal support during the past few years. He has helped me through some trials and tribulations, and this book probably would not have been completed without his support.

Thanks to my friends and discussion partners in the Spurgeon-Lewis consortium. J.R.R. Tolkien and C.S. Lewis had their group, the Inklings, and I am fortunate to be part of a special, once-in-a-lifetime group of dedicated, Christian men who are a modern-day Inklings. Rev. Ross, Rev. Marcus, Rev. Dale, Dave, Doug, Jay, John, and others have been great discussion partners as we work through life challenges, theology, and ministry together.

Thank you to Athena Dean Holtz, the owner of Redemption Press, for your support and for arranging for the Columbia Evangelical Seminary imprint. I recommend that any prospective Christian authors check out Redemption Press to see if it fits their publishing needs.

Michelle Booth was a fantastic and thorough editor and proofreader. Many, many thanks to Michelle for her diligent work!

The board of Columbia Evangelical Seminary: Mike Buchanon, Rick Luiten, Stuart Young, Brad Stewart, Randy Weiss, and Rick Walston. In particular, The Board of Regents: Phil Fernandes, Steve Rowe, Brent Atkison, and Marcus Kelly have been especially supportive of me and of my work.

My mom, Virginia Odell-Eliason, and my dad, Ken Hein, for raising me to love God. My dad's time in seminary during my elementary school years played a large role in kindling a higher level of interest in the things of God. My step-father, Mark Eliason, has also been a great influence. He gave me some books from his time studying religion at Pacific Lutheran University, and those books were very influential in fanning my interest in the specific areas covered in this book.

I want to give special thanks my wife Christine for her support. My degree programs and work on books has taken a huge amount of time, and she has been a strong encourager.

Our son, Ephraim, has been the joy of our life since he joined our family in 2008. Academic degrees and books take quite a bit of time, and I have tried to be both a good academic and a great father, despite sacrificing family time to work on these things. If only one person reads and finds value from this book, I hope it is Ephraim.

Preface

FOR THOSE WHO WANT TO skip to the heart of the book, go ahead and start with the prologue and skip this preface. For those who have an interest in academics, you may find this preface of value. It details some of my thoughts and background on the overall topic that I left out of the heart of the book.

During the twentieth century, a Romanian scholar by the name of Mircea Eliade established himself as an expert in the areas of comparative religion and the history of religions. He pioneered some groundbreaking approaches toward understanding religious experience and behavior, and his observations are still relevant and widely discussed when studying religious history. Using an approach to religious experience similar to Rudolf Otto's, Eliade popularized the foundation for today's modern concepts of sacred space, sacred time, axis mundi, hierophany, and several other ideas. However, in his popular writings, he did not apply his research and concepts to develop, clarify, or espouse any particular theology, preferring instead to classify and understand religious behavior in general. In fact, though coming from an Orthodox Christian background, there is much speculation and debate over his personal beliefs and views on theology, with conclusions on the topic ranging from pantheistic religion to universalism to inclusionism to Orthodox Christianity. I don't claim to know what his personally held beliefs were. However, the quality, discussion, and broad use of his work speak for itself. Even scholars who disagree with his analysis acknowledge his impact.

On a scholarly level, I embrace some (not all) of his ideas, and I intend to apply my personal, academic interpretation of his foundational concepts to the study that follows. My indebtedness to Eliade and others in this field will be clear to anyone who is familiar with this area of academics. His work, and those like him, has its detractors. I'm familiar with the critiques, some of which I in turn wholly or partially agree with, and others I disagree with. Such is the nature of academia. As an early student who found portions of a particular theologian's writing unpalatable, a professor once said to me, "I expect you to eat the meat and discard the bones." It was sage advice. Since that day I have attempted to apply that philosophy to all of my work, including this one.

As an unapologetic theist of the Christian variety, I apply many of Eliade's ideas and methods, with my own spin, as interpretative tools for understanding certain aspects of religious behavior found in the Bible. I make no apology to either the academics who recoil at the thought of applying neutral scholarly work as a tool for specific religious interpretation and theology, nor do I make excuses to any Christians who fear the application of ideas that did not originate within the bounds of conservative, evangelical Christendom. With that said, I'm presenting this book for your consumption because I believe it's important for the Christian church to embrace and proactively live according to the principles of Christocentrism laid out here. That's not a statement of arrogance—the conclusions derived over the course of this study are the same ideas scripture already laid out previously. As such, they did not originate with me and I lay no claim to them as my own. Rather, I am attempting to bring the core, biblical theology of Christian living into greater clarity in a Christian society that I believe has largely lost focus on the essentials and gotten tangled up in the peripherals. I take a unique approach to this particular topic. This approach is my own (hopefully guided by God), but the core ideas and theology are taken directly from scripture. You will find no secret or new theology revealed here, just a new and fascinating approach to ideas Christians have already been exposed to. The route I've taken to expose and expound upon my conclusions may consist of paths that seem unfamiliar and strange to most Christians, but in the end, I think you'll find that it fits. It fits, not because I've fashioned some fancy, cross-disciplinary application of historical religious analysis with Christian theology, but because it's true.

As we approach this topic, keep in mind that the "irrational" ancient symbols, myths, and rituals (such as standing stones), are not as mysterious and inexplicable as one might think. They all participate in an organized, understandable system of expression and communication (a symbolic pattern) that pre-existed the systematic theology we enjoy today. The ancient people didn't have access to the complex, precise religious terminology created over the centuries of modern theology's refinement. In fact, much of the earliest foundation of the ancient patterns of thought and behavior comes from a time before written language was prevalent. However, before writing was common, people enjoyed extremely effective religious communication using rituals and symbols.[1] For example, ancient myths about creation were more than a telling of an entertaining, epic tale; these myths established the paradigm for human existence, religious behavior, and ancient metaphysics. They also helped to establish social boundaries and controls.[2] Just because our ancestors didn't write the ancient concepts in a technical written volume spanning several hundred pages, it doesn't mean that their concepts weren't effectively communicable or precise. It just means that those of us living in today's modern context are so reliant on our current forms of communication that we have to work harder to recognize and understand these different, older forms of communication. Ancient people's use of symbol, myth, and ritual did indeed represent a well-developed, established, and understandable system of religious thought.[3]

Furthermore, given that Christianity holds the Bible as God-breathed and God-inspired,[4] the myths, symbols, and rituals found in the stories of scripture are not accidental inclusions; they are there for a reason. Christianity teaches that the Bible is a timeless book for all people from all cultures. The people who lived in the cultures and times of the Bible—whose very lives comprised the famous stories of scripture—did not share the modern mindset most Christians have today. Because of this, we must remember the modern context we live in today is different from the context that framed the lives of people of the Bible. As Christians, we must strive to understand the fullness of scripture *in the context of when, where, why, and to whom it was written.*

Understanding the Bible in its full context is part of the role of hermeneutics. While several biblical passages are self-explanatory within their immediate context, interpretation of many others requires due diligence and careful attention to a far broader and less obvious context that includes culture, time, geography, and more. It's easy to focus on the simple passages and not dedicate time to understand the more difficult sections. However, Jesus never excused people for their misunderstandings of scripture because they didn't want to expend effort. He did not tell people only to follow the passage they understood easily and then not to bother with the ones that required effort and thought. Instead, Jesus actually scolded the religious experts of his time for their lack of understanding. The apostle Paul also expressed the need to expend effort in understanding scripture when he wrote a letter to Timothy encouraging him to be "a workman who does not need to be ashamed, accurately handling the word of truth" (2 Timothy 2:15b). Peter embraced diligence and scholarship with regard to understanding, presenting, and defending the faith when stating that we should be "ready to make a defense to everyone who asks you to give an account for the hope that is in you" (1 Peter 3:15b). The instructions to Titus on qualifications for an elder include "holding fast the faithful word . . . so that he will be able both to exhort in sound doctrine and to refute those who contradict" (Titus 1:9).

Even though some passages require careful study, the basic, foundational truths of Christianity as expressed in the Bible are clear and easy to understand. After all, we read and understand that we cannot save ourselves through our own work. We have all sinned, and the finished work of Christ provides the only hope for salvation. "For all have sinned" (Romans 3:23), "the wages of sin is death" (Romans 6:23), and "no one comes to the Father but through me [Jesus]" (John 14:6) are easy passages to understand. However, the topics we are studying are some of the non-foundational passages, and these often require a bit more work on our part. By taking a careful look at certain specific aspects of scripture, and by applying an educated approach with thoughtful analysis, we'll be able understand their subtleties.

All people apply a context for filtering claims of truth: a worldview. There are no exceptions; there are only differences with regard to what specific worldview someone holds. My worldview is Christian theism, and so this work is done from that perspective. However, the goal of this book is not to make an argument for the validity of Christian theism. I did not write this as an apologetic work. I assume that the primary audience of this book is comprised of people who hold to some variation of the worldview of Christian theism. If the reader does not embrace this view, I believe there is still significant value contained in this book for you; however, this it is not intended to be an argument for Christian theism. Those who seek an understanding of why one might consider Christian theism to be the correct worldview would do well to read books like Francis Schaeffer's *The God Who is There*, J. P. Moreland's *Scaling the Secular City*, Ravi Zacharias's *Jesus Among Other Gods*, or Norman

Geisler's *Christian Apologetics*. For those who are brave readers, you might consider any of William Lane Craig's books related to God and time.

One final note: I wrote this book over the course of ten years. After I had already written my first few drafts and was late in the editing stage (which took a few years), my senior pastor introduced me to a book called *The Unseen Realm* written by Dr. Michael Heiser. This book is a fantastic example of attempting to understand certain passages in the Bible from the context of the people of scripture based on language, culture, and solid hermeneutics. I can't recommend this book highly enough. Dr. Heiser's scholarship is excellent, and I believe we share a similar goal with regard to understanding the scriptures in the context of when they were written. This does not imply that he would agree with or endorse my work, but anyone who has read both his work and mine will notice some similarities in approach. If you finish this book and find the approach to understanding the Bible interesting, I suggest purchasing a copy of *The Unseen Realm* and giving it a try. It's a bit denser than this work, but it's well worth the effort. I have given copies of this book to multiple people and have preached sermons based in part on his book (as well as my own research), and it always leads to great conversations.

Prologue

"IT'S TIME TO GO NOW."

The man looked over at his wife to see if she heard him as they finished loading up a donkey with their belongings. They were leaving a life of comfort and luxury, and now there were headed off to start over somewhere else. At least they still had each other.

"I wonder what's out there," said the wife looking off into the distance.

They didn't know exactly where they were headed. They were leaving the only place they ever knew, and the lands outside were a mystery to them. They did know that life was going to be much more difficult now. The freedom they lived in was significantly diminished, and life would be much more of a struggle in the years ahead. But that wouldn't be the hardest part.

Turning to look at someone standing quietly behind him, the man asked, "Will I see you again?"

"Yes," came the reply from his old friend. "We will see each other from time to time. I will be there when you need me. But things will be different."

"I know," came the man's reply, "but I think I'm only just beginning to understand how different. I don't know if I can comprehend how hard it will be. I'm already starting to feel the change."

"No, in truth, you don't know yet," replied the friend gently. "However, it won't last forever," he said with deep conviction. "And remember: God will provide."

"I believe you," said the man earnestly.

Tears welled up in both of their eyes as they hugged good-bye. The man looked around one last time, making a mental picture of this place. Then he took his wife by her hand, and together they began finding their way down from the lush mountain valley and toward the lowlands below. They would never return, but God had a plan.

Introduction

IN THE MIDDLE OF A vast expanse of farmland, a long, lonely road divides the green pastures. Cows graze lazily behind a small fence on one side of the road, seemingly oblivious to the constant flow of traffic that seems to be disproportionately heavy for a quiet, rural area just a few miles outside of Salisbury. Cars, vans, and tour buses deposit people from all over the world in a hard, paved parking lot, which stands in stark contrast to the soft, green fields surrounding it. Visitors find their way between the vehicles and head toward a place of solemn mystery. They walk around, talk in hushed voices, and take several pictures. Many stop to ask other tourists—strangers all—to take pictures of them against this backdrop so they can have a photographic souvenir. Their visit to this mysterious monument forms a lasting memory. In years to come, they will ponder it, talk about it, and tell their descendants stories about it. This experience is part of each visitor, part of the wealth of significant experiences that shape a person, even though a basic description of this location doesn't seem that impressive. After all, it's just a bunch of rocks, sitting in a field, in the middle of otherwise normal and unspectacular farmland. The same description could be given to any number of places, none of which most people would remember, let alone travel to. Yet, for anyone who has visited Stonehenge, it is so much more.

Thousands of miles to the southeast, an armada of cruise ships docks at an island off the coast of Mexico's Yucatan peninsula. Once again, thousands of tourists from all over the world have come to see something spectacular and fascinating. Leaving their massive floating cities, they take small boats to the mainland and then climb into the rows of tour buses waiting to take them south along the coast toward a relatively deserted location. As soon as the vehicles reach the gravel parking lot at their destination, tourists stream out of the air-conditioned buses into high heat and heavy humidity. Following the signs, they walk along a dirt road leading into the ancient Mayan ruins of Tulum. Tour guides regale them with stories of the mysterious Mayan civilization while wandering among the ancient stone buildings. Iguanas sunning themselves on nearby rocks watch as many of the tourists choose to swim in the warm, clear Caribbean waters or sun themselves on the small beach at the base of the cliff under the watchful eyes of the old, ruined village stretched out along the top. Near the center of the cliff top stands the most recognizable feature of the village: the ancient temple. It is a large, tall, pyramid-shaped building—the tallest of any nearby—and it sits in a place of prominence as it rises above the rest of the abandoned village. Crowds gather before it and listen raptly to the tales of mystical rituals and sacrifice. As they make their way past the souvenir shops back toward the parking lot, descendants of the ancient Mayans re-enact a ritual common to the lives of their ancestors. They climb a tall pole, sing, and dance, hoping to entertain and educate the many visitors that pass by and stop to watch. Like Stonehenge, it is a place where modern humans meet the mysterious past, and it leaves a mark on those who visit.

In the Middle East, visitors and religious faithful climb mountains of shared Jewish, Christian, and Islamic history, and in doing so, they retrace the footsteps of ancient heroes and prophets. The Mounts of Sinai, Tabor, and Zion are classic travel destinations for those interested in the religious aspects of what many refer to as the Holy Land. For curious visitors, these mountains are more than just large, elevated swaths of land raised high by the ancient forces of tectonic collision; they impart a sense of something else, something more than just rock and soil. Whatever that something is, it touches human experience today even as it did long ago for the early forefathers of the theistic faiths, and it evokes much of the same experience: the solemn, the mysterious, and the sacred.

Encountering the Sacred

The impact of these experiences on visitors is not necessarily isolated to a particular cultural inheritance, geographic locale, expression of faith, or any other method that distinguishes and separates people. Humanity in general is open to and deeply affected by sacred places, spirituality, and religion. The ancient, sacred locations just mentioned are only a few examples out of many thousands found throughout the world. In every place that modern humans discover these sacred sites, people venerate and visit them as places of historical, anthropological, and mystical value. For some people, the mystical or spiritual aspect makes them feel uneasy, particularly theists who don't share the same religious views as the ancient people who constructed these sites. Nonetheless, these monuments exist as evidence of prolific religious thought and behavior among the generations of people that lived and died long before our time. While some people may view these places strictly as historical footnotes of religions long since dead or dormant, other modern people still value them as relevant to their spiritual lives. Stonehenge is an example of this: many modern druids and neo-pagans revere the sacred site as a place of power, particularly during the solstices. While Stonehenge is unique in terms of recognition and preservation, there are hundreds of stone circles and megaliths[5] found throughout Europe, and many more found throughout the rest of the world. Scholars from various fields debate their exact use and value ad nauseam; however, in ages past, people clearly valued these sites for religious purposes (as well as for more mundane and practical purposes). The myriad of mystical locations throughout the world is a testament to the value, prevalence, and power of the supernatural experience in ancient cultures, even though many people living today don't generally value these religious experiences, practices, or rituals to the same extent. Instead, modern expressions of faith often focus more on the logical, rational, and methodical aspects of faith. While this shift in mindset is understandable given society's increasing emphasis on scientific methodologies, Christians should not forget that the people in the stories of the Bible probably found the very essence of interaction with God to be very mystical and seemingly non-rational. For example, the burning bush and the voice of God speaking to Moses on Mt. Sinai probably seemed a bit odd if viewed strictly within the rational, logical, and philosophical framework many people embrace today. The heroes of the Christian faith certainly experienced mystical situations that went far beyond a list of rules, guidelines, and strictly rational experiences. They experienced the supernatural: Abraham hosted heavenly visitors (Genesis 18). Elijah called to God and fire came down to consume a sacrifice (1 Kings 18). Peter walked on water (Matthew 14), witnessed miraculous healings (Acts 3), and observed the Transfiguration (Mark 9). Paul encountered the resurrected Christ on the road to Damascus, and later he wrote about what appears to be his direct experience of heaven (Acts 9; 2 Corinthians 12:2-4). A comprehensive list of similar experiences in the Bible would be enormous. These heroes of our typically logical and rational faith appear to have valued and embraced these mystical experiences despite how uncommon, unusual, and unscientific these occurrences were. We should recognize these experiences as significant to both the ancient people in the Bible and to those of us who read the Bible today.

But, as we start to look at the symbols, myths, and rituals in the Bible, let's start by making it clear we're *not* discussing some secret, hidden doctrine or new theology. When a teacher claims his doctrine is available only to the initiated, select few, or when the doctrine claims to have a hidden, secret meaning revealed via personal revelation, mystical practices, or deciphered codes, then that is a big, bold warning sign of a teaching that is *not* biblically true. Don't walk—run away—and don't return! We're certainly not headed in that direction with this study. Nevertheless, the ancient myths, symbols, and rituals we may not fully understand are indeed part of the Bible that God has given to us, so we are going to analyze these unfamiliar and entertaining topics so that we can understand them. Grab your favorite drink, settle into a comfortable chair, and let's start this fascinating journey!

❧ CHAPTER 1: ☙

History and Mystery

MY WIFE AND I SPENT part of the 2009 Christmas season vacationing with some friends from church. At this point of the trip, we were spending time in the gorgeous Austrian town of Salzburg. We've probably spent more vacation time in Salzburg than anywhere else, and we love the Altstadt (Old Town) with its charming feel, picturesque buildings, and great restaurants, not to mention lots of history. One of the many places we like to visit is St. Peter's cemetery, which served as inspiration for the tension-filled cemetery hideout scene in *The Sound of Music* (one of the few musicals I enjoyed as a child). I've probably visited this cemetery four or five times, and we always follow the same path: we enter the cemetery near the funicular that leads up to the Hohensalzburg fortress, and then we leave on the other side where it exits into a large, empty square. To be honest, Chris (my wife) and I always found the square largely uninteresting. It seems so plain compared to the rest of the old town, especially after walking through the ornate burial grounds. Although nice public squares like this one are noticeably different from what we have in the Pacific Northwest, in Europe it seems like just another large square with no distinguishing features. So, on this particular day, once again we walked right through the square and quickly made our way to other locations we thought were more interesting. Later in the day, after meeting up with our friends and telling them about the places we visited, they told us about a restaurant just off that square that may be one of the oldest in Europe. This restaurant, Stiftskeller St. Peter, boasts the honor of having hosted Charlemagne on his visit in 803—more than 1,200 years ago! Being that Charlemagne was an important historical ruler who helped to usher in the Carolingian renaissance and implemented education reform (a rarity back then), we made a point to go back to that square and visit the restaurant that very evening. We were able to get seats in the lower part of the restaurant at what was the narrowest table I have ever seen. It was little more than an elevated bench, and the seating was awkward. However, the food was good and the atmosphere was fantastic. It turned out to be a fun and memorable experience.

Despite our previous time spent in Salzburg, Chris and I had no clue the restaurant we passed in the square (several times) was anything other than an ordinary dining establishment. Without the help of someone who offered a fresh perspective, we would have remained ignorant of the presence and significance of the restaurant, and we would have missed a great experience on our trip. Sometimes a fresh perspective opens the door to a new and impactful experience.

Scripture's Symbolic Journey

We can say the same thing about our journeys through the stories of scripture. Sometimes we need help to make the most of our time spent there. That is why we have discussion groups, study guides, and commentaries. Personally, I already have a lot of knowledge about the Bible. I have several degrees in religion and theology, and I serve as a seminary president. However, I still attend small discussion groups with people who come from a variety of backgrounds and experiences. Sometimes

I am often the only one with any formal training in Christian thought, but I always learn something from the perspective and life experiences of everyone in the group. Hearing a different perspective can be very valuable. The same is true in our studies of the Bible. When we read, we don't want to miss something during our personal, biblical travels that might offer a rich and impactful experience to us. Unfortunately, many of us don't immediately recognize the myths, symbols, and rituals in the Bible, and even when we do, we may not fully grasp their context or significance. It's easy for modern believers to dismiss older religious experiences due to our modern lack of understanding and the assumption that those older practices or perspectives are no longer relevant to us today.

However, whether the religious experience is one belonging to ages past or is common to a modern expression of faith, the basic characteristics of religious experience are universal in many ways. This does not mean that all religions are true or accurate—that's impossible given their vast contradictions and antithetical positions. But despite the differences, we can say that people who practice religion are familiar with the experience of *something else* that transcends mundane existence and points to a higher aspect of reality that exceeds the one they're used to. This experience of that *something else* often inspires people toward a lifetime of spiritual pursuit and religious devotion.[6]

This transcendent encounter is one of the key, universal aspects of all religion.[7] Rudolf Otto, the famous theologian and respected scholar of comparative religions, analyzed how people from various religious backgrounds encountered the sacred. In *Das Heilige* he described five common elements found in the experience of this transcendent, sacred *something else*.[8] His work provided fertile, academic ground for new ways of examining and learning about comparative religion and history. Other famous religious scholars, such as Mircea Eliade, built upon this foundation with considerable skill and penetrating insight, and Eliade's influence remains evident in many of the studies that followed.[9] However, his research focused on academics and did not offer much in the way of theological commentary or practical application.

The academic, impersonal mindset may seem natural for Christian analysis given that Christianity bases its beliefs on inspired, inerrant scriptures that offer clear, rational guidelines for how to experience and interpret life. For some modern Christians, their black-and-white faith, and the common Sunday school emphasis on lists of "dos" and "do-nots" can seem a bit at odds with mystical experiences that may be difficult to understand and express. Since the Greek scholarly traditions influenced much of Christianity's earliest and most influential approaches to theology, which relied heavily on rational, logical, and philosophical approaches, this is not surprising.[10]

However, consider this: if modern Christianity is completely understandable and rational with regard to the experiential aspects of the human relationship with God, then it is an abject failure. For surely the flawed, finite human cannot fully understand and describe the presence and experience of the perfect, infinite God. The rapture of worship, the transcendence of beauty, and the receipt of true, unconditional love all point to something transcendent that is impossible, not just difficult, to fully comprehend and describe in rational terms. God is more than just the logical, philosophical deduction of human observation, and as a result, our finite, logical, rational language cannot to describe Him in a full and comprehensive manner.

By virtue of humanity's finite nature, descriptions of God attempt to reduce the infinite, mysterious divine to the limits of what our minds can comprehend.[11] As a result, people often use poetic and symbolic expressions to talk about God when attempting to communicate concepts that naturally transcend the limitations of normal speech.[12] When interacting with a symbolic expression as opposed to a concrete, finite expression, a person can experience the concepts in a different (and hopefully more effective) way.[13] Famous theologian Dietrich Bonhoeffer explained that symbolic representation of a deep concept is what often enables the true, underlying meaning to touch an individual in a unique and powerful way.[14] Popular Christian author and counselor John Eldredge talked about mythic-styled stories helping people understand truth with their heart as opposed to having merely an intellectual understanding.[15] J. R. R. Tolkien believed that sometimes myth was the only way to effectively communicate about transcendent truth.[16] In many ways, it's similar to how Jesus used parables to teach concepts to his audience in unique, impactful ways. He presented concrete truth by using stories and symbols. This allowed the listeners (and today's readers) to approach the same topic in a unique and stimulating way. I was once at a training session led by a former Southern Baptist preacher, and he used the phrase (with a great Texas drawl), "You have to use your SpongeBob imagination!" It made everyone laugh, it lightened the mood, and it did force us to consciously engage a different part of our brains for that portion of the training. Metaphors, similes, parables, and symbols all help people approach topics from a fresh perspective.

When trying to understand symbolic communication, such as those found in the Bible, people commonly question if a particular item is literally true or if it is strictly symbolic instead. This supposed dilemma is very common when dealing with religion. For example, look at the numerous references throughout the Bible to God conquering a sea beast that is referred to as Leviathan or Rahab (Job 26:12-13, Psalm 74:13-14, Psalm 89:10, Isaiah 27:1, Isaiah 51:9, others). Due to the context of use, it appears symbolic in at least a few of the passages. However, does that mean that God never actually subdued a chaotic, evil sea monster? Not necessarily. He may have. Similarly, was the Tree of Life in the Garden of Eden symbolic? Yes, without a doubt. The symbolism is obvious for anyone with an eye to see it (and we'll look at this specific example in detail later in the book). However, that does not mean that it was not also an actual, literal tree. I believe it was both. It is possible for something to be simultaneously literal *and* symbolic.[17] After all, the root prefix of symbol is "sym-," which is equivalent to "syn-," both of which generally mean "together, with, at the same time,"[18] *neither to the exclusion of the other.* As we progress through many of the symbols in the Bible, it's important to keep this in mind.

Historical Missteps

Despite the pervasiveness of symbolic communication in the Bible, quality analysis of the interaction between Christianity and ancient religious practices is rare in our modern society, although this is not entirely unique to current generations. Historically, Christendom adopted some common approaches to govern its interaction with older symbols, myths, and rituals. Despite attempts to preserve the faith and protect believers from error, none of the approaches has been particularly successful.

First, the easiest and most common approach was to ignore many symbolic expressions of faith altogether. This often happened unintentionally out of ignorance. For example, most modern people don't generally carve twenty-ton blocks of stone and place them in a local park for use in religious rituals. This in turn limits modern people's exposure to this particular expression of spirituality and may cause them to question the modern relevance of this ancient practice. When Christians come across a similar symbol in the Bible, they may not notice it since they can't really relate to it. This probably happens more often than people realize. Symbolic expressions are often subconsciously ignored as the mind does not have a good frame of reference by which to process them.

Second, the early church started two thousand years ago during a time when many of these symbols and practices were still somewhat common. The easiest approach for the early church was to deliberately eradicate all of these seemingly mystical and irrational practices—and to a certain extent, that is exactly what happened.[19] As the early church fathers strove to define and codify the Christian faith, they relied heavily on rationalism and logic at the expense of the mystical. In many ways, it was a good approach for them to take given the circumstances of their time. However, even in our modern-day lives, we must be careful not to overemphasize rationalism and logic to the point of inappropriately excluding the non-rational aspects of religious experience. This is part of what happened over the course of church history: the emphasis on rationalism and logic as a means to define, establish, and defend the faith left little room for the areas of religious experience that did not fit neatly into that mindset.[20] As a result, we are left with a void of easily accessible writing and teaching on the topic.

Another series of failures lies with Christendom's attempt at assimilation over the past two thousand years. In several cases, Christian leaders attempted to morph common pagan religious behaviors into something more acceptable, sometimes attributing parts of older pagan legends to more recent Christian heroes. For example, look at the legends regarding Saint George. He was probably an important historical person who lived about seventeen hundred years ago in various locations between Israel and the Black Sea, and eventually he became a martyr after refusing to recant his Christian faith.[21] Stories about him grew over the years, and eventually the truth about his life became more of a legend. Eventually the legend incorporated ancient mythological patterns commonly ascribed to the heroes in old pagan tales. This made him more relatable to the people familiar with the pagan legends. The stories of him battling and defeating a dragon clearly originate from the preceding, non-Christian religious traditions in the eastern Mediterranean region and probably have nothing to do with literal reality.[22] Similar things happened with missionaries in the Americas when they interacted with the Mayan population. There are significant questions if some of the "saints" established in the Americas were simply re-branded, pre-existing

Mayan deities changed to match the saint model brought by the Catholic church. If true, this appropriation and re-branding may have happened either deliberately as conscious decisions made by the missionaries or subconsciously by the people to whom they witnessed.[23] Assimilation, whether intentional or coincidental, was a tricky business leading to unpredictable results and questionable long-term value.

Sometimes Christian leaders avoided assimilation and condemned the ancient myths, symbols, and rituals outright. In some of these cases, the locals changed the condemned practices into something a bit more palatable and easier for the clergy to accept, even though the changes were not necessarily Christian. This happened throughout Europe as pagan traditions and local witchcraft encountered the dominant Christian culture. The resulting pressure from the clash of beliefs forced change.[24] The example of the Benandanti cult in Italy demonstrates the ineffectiveness of this artificial change. In this specific example, the local pagan beliefs, which were considered to be witchcraft by the local church, clearly conflicted with church rules. As a result, the locals changed their pagan rituals just enough to fall into the superficial categorization of being "Christianized." This allowed them to preserve some of their superstitions and beliefs while avoiding witch hunts and the Inquisition—but only for a short time. The benefit of superficial change did not last. The cult's façade of Christianity eventually fell away as it returned to its deep pagan undercurrents.[25]

The questionable approach of assimilation led some prominent thinkers to consider Christianity as a religion of deliberately false pretenses that was adapted from pre-existing cultures. For example, Thomas Paine, one of America's founding fathers and a signer of the Declaration of Independence, wrote that he considered Christianity to be a fraudulent manipulation of ancient mythologies. He believed its goal was to gain money and power.[26] While as a Christian I obviously don't agree with Paine's view, a cynical view of church history, particularly with its attempts at assimilation, could lead to that same erroneous conclusion he embraced. Religious assimilation or superficial change proved to be better in theory than in practice.

Today we're left with a society conditioned by Christendom's varied approaches to symbols, myths, and rituals. Because of this, modern Christians who try to understand the symbolic religious expressions in the Bible start off with a handicap compared to the people who lived during the time the scriptures were written. This is not an easy situation to overcome in our modern thinking, but we're going to address that with our study. As we continue looking at this topic from a fresh, renewed perspective, we have to start by establishing the context necessary to understand the beliefs and actions of people so far removed from us.

~5 CHAPTER 2: ॐ

Context

I WAS THIRTY-TWO YEARS OLD when I visited a concentration camp for the first time since I was an infant. For most of my life up until that point, I thought I was fairly well-educated on the Holocaust; I thought I understood it well enough. Though born in Germany, I grew up in the United States and received the standard education offered in the U.S. school system about the infamous Nazi persecution. Through the first three decades of my life, the writings of victims like Anne Frank, documentaries like *Blood from a Stone*, movies like *Schindler's List*, and all the other easily accessible resources seemed adequate to convey a sense of the evil that the Nazis inflicted on so many people.

One holiday season Chris and I decided to return to Germany in order to visit the world-famous Christmas markets. We knew that it would be an incredible, memorable, and joyful experience (it was all that and more). However, since Christmas is about the significance of the arrival of the Christ, I felt it was important to take time to witness some of the history of the depravity of humanity—the very thing that Jesus came to free us from. With that in mind, on our first morning in Germany we gathered with some other tourists in the middle of the

München Christmas market. Soon we departed the fun, bright, and uplifting square in front of the Neues Rathaus to visit the bleak, dark, and dreadful Dachau concentration camp. We didn't fully understand how the visit would affect us—at least not yet.

I cannot adequately describe the experience of the concentration camp with words. I'm not sure that I even fully understand what experiencing it did to me. Books, movies, and conversations don't do justice to the topic. The sheer evil of such a place is overwhelming and confusing, even for someone who intellectually acknowledges the utter depravity of humanity. The abuse, torture, and murder of people, simply because they belonged to a targeted group, is a horror that remains inexplicable in its intractable evil. As purely evil as Dachau was, in some ways it wasn't as bad as the true extermination camps like Krakow and Auschwitz. That says something about the force of evil in that place. Chris and I both came away changed, and the experience has not left us. I hope it never does.

The following summer we were at a company picnic for Chris's job. In the middle of a clearing in a local park, a giant blow-up slide was set up for the kids to use. One of the adults in attendance stood at the foot of the slide and ensured the kids behaved and stayed safe. Someone walking by asked him if he was the "slide Nazi." He grinned, answered in the affirmative, and people standing around chuckled. As we drove home from the picnic later that day, Chris explained that the passerby's slide Nazi comment really bothered her. In her conversations with people since visiting the concentration camp, and with hearing many lighthearted comments similar to slide Nazi, she realized our visit to the concentration camp radically altered her personal context for understanding the use of that term. Once she learned—really learned—about Nazis and the Holocaust, she could no longer approach certain things as casually as she once could. Neither could I. Our personal context shifted from basic, intellectual knowledge of a historical event to a context that was more rich, experiential, and deep. Even then, our context for understanding the Nazi persecution is significantly inferior to the contextual understanding possessed by anyone who actually experienced that persecution, either in hiding from the Nazis or in the camps themselves.

For Chris, this experience helped open her eyes to importance of engaging in the pursuit of context. Oftentimes people do not realize that the understanding they think they have about an unfamiliar topic is actually very limited and insufficient. Context is the fulcrum that enables unwitting ignorance to begin the change toward true knowledge.

Identifying Context

Everyone makes judgments and guesses based on the way we view the world as individuals. Even though we embrace the framework of Christian theism, when evaluating unfamiliar things we encounter in ancient religion, we must apply the appropriate ancient cultural context when we try to understand the older beliefs. For example, while Christians do not believe the same thing as the Zoroastrians of ancient Persia, in order to understand their Zoroastrian myths, symbols, and rituals, we must be able to understand and apply their ideological framework. Their framework was not Christian theism, so we have to adjust accordingly if we are to gain understanding.

We should note that the ancient people's widespread and perpetual religious lifestyle (as demonstrated by their myths, symbols, and rituals) demonstrates just how centrally important and real experiences of the divine were *to them* (even if many modern people don't agree). They occupied a central place and guided their lives.[27]

In general, ancient people believed that human existence itself came about via the direct will and act of the divine. They also believed that most or all aspects of life were intrinsically religious and that humanity could only reach the fullness of its potential through corresponding religiosity.[28] This was not specific to the older cultures of the Middle

East we read about in the scriptures. Regardless of where people lived throughout history, the vast majority of them were religious or spiritual. Even though the *particulars* of the various ancient religious behaviors differed between cultures and belief systems, the basic *patterns* of religious behavior were very similar to each other. The ancient people believed their religious experiences were real, and these real experiences contained supreme meaning and value for living.

Whether or not their specific truth claims regarding reality and religious experience were actually correct does not matter in this context (and as a Christian, I generally think they were incorrect). When trying to understand the practices of those who went before us, *it's their view that matters for the purpose of establishing context*, not our modern opinions. This provides us with an important perspective to consider with regard to cultural context: if an ancient society treated a certain religious practice with supreme value and reverence, we must define our framework for understanding the intent and meaning communicated by that practice according to the ancient society's supreme value and reverence for it. Therefore, in our analysis we must be careful not to diminish the value of a specific religious practice simply because we do not use or agree with that same practice in our culture today.

Interpreting and determining the appropriate cultural context also involves some other elements. We must consider more than just the immediate, obvious culture; we need to account for its surrounding influences as well. For example, the physical environment can play a large part in an expression of mythology and symbolism. The symbolism found in desert, arctic, and jungle cultures may differ in the *particulars*, although their overall *patterns* may be similar. For example, the metaphysical particulars of rain mythologies could vary for cultures living in the dry Arabian Desert (four inches of rain per year) as opposed to those living in the very wet Hoh Rainforest on the Olympic Peninsula in the Pacific Northwest (more than 144 inches of rain per year).

An individual culture's history will also have a significant impact, as will the cultures with whom they come in contact. If two different groups of people live in close proximity and interact with one another, you can expect to see significant interaction between their religions, symbols, and myths. If Culture A conquers Culture B, then both cultures A and B experience cultural change on some level—both the conquered and the conqueror impart some portion of their cultural influences to each other as they mingle over time. Military conquest does not necessarily equate to ideological conquest.

Environment, history, and neighboring cultures are a few examples of some elements that affect overall cultural context for ancient religious practices. Identifying all the relevant variables is outside the scope of our study, so we just need to remember that cultural context is not static. It can change with time, setting, and influences. While we do not need to alter our personal contexts with regard to determining truth (Christians remain Christian theists), we do need to keep other contexts in mind when interacting with different belief systems if we hope to understand them.

As We Begin in Earnest

We are about to delve into topics that have intrigued people for centuries. The religious symbols, myths, and rituals described in the Bible match general patterns used throughout the historical world. As we progress through this study, we will see that many modern people still unknowingly use the same patterns today (including some of you reading this book). We will learn about many of the symbols, myths, and rituals used in lands both known and unknown to the biblical authors. This will help us understand the broader scope of human religious behavior in order to discern the *pattern* of the symbol or ritual even though the *particulars* (doctrinal truths) differ.

Keeping in mind some of Christianity's struggles with symbol, myth, and ritual through the years, we have to begin by making sure we don't continue the mistake of overlooking the existence of some key biblical patterns. During our scripture readings, it is easy for us to settle into a familiar pattern and fail to notice certain things we missed previously. As we learn about these patterns, some of them will immediately be clear and obvious, but some other patterns we identify will be subtler. Once we have established the existence of those symbols, we will analyze them within their immediate cultural context at that point in history, including how people used them as part of their belief system. Then, as we analyze the truth claims that are either explicit or implicit in these practices, we'll do it within the context of Christian theism. Christianity holds to the Bible as the inspired,[29] inerrant[30] word of God, and this will be the measure for any truth or value found in these ancient practices. Additionally, since the Bible is "life's guidebook" for all people of all times, it can also provide proper lifestyle context for how to apply what we learn. Let's begin!

CHAPTER 3:

What Lies Beneath

MY FAMILY WAS ENJOYING A nice, warm day, at least by the standards of someone who grew up in the Seattle area. The sun was out, the sky was blue, and the day was full of promise. However, our local guide in Belize thought it a bit chilly, and he was fighting off a cold. Apparently, he considered eighty degrees, sunny, and dry to be too cool and unpleasant for Belize, and he said this was the time of year when people down there fell ill. Talk about different perspectives—Seattle, which has relatively mild seasons, was half that warm when we left, and Belize seemed very hot to me. Regardless, my family travelled deep into the mountains of Belize enjoying both the weather and the very striking scenery.

After a long drive, we finally arrived at a small jungle outpost. We climbed out of the van we had been riding in and began to travel on foot along a jungle path. We were keeping keen watch for the spiders, snakes, and other nasty jungle creatures. We were absolutely convinced they stalked us from barely beyond the edge of our vision. Warily we walked with cautious eyes alert for movement from the strange jungle surrounding us until the mystery and adventure of what we were about to experience distracted us from our misperception of the insect-infested jungle. As it turns out, I see more spiders on a typical trip into my garage than I did that entire day in the jungle.

Soon we arrived at the edge of a lazy, green, jungle river, and the sight astounded us. It was just as beautiful as you might imagine, and the mysterious jungle setting made me think that Indiana Jones would feel right at home in that location. On the far side of the river, a tall cliff rose as an impassable barrier while the river meandered leisurely along its base. On our side, we stood in a small clearing formed of rocks and sand at the edge of the river. Large trees leaned in over this small beach and provided us with shade. Holding tight to our float tubes, we followed our guide into the calm river and began adjusting to the water temperature (which was surprisingly comfortable and warm). Looking back upstream, we could see where the river emerged from underground out of the cliff. It looked as if the earth was releasing water from its mysterious depths up onto the surface of the world, but only for a short while. Turning to look downstream, we saw the reason for our visit: the river ahead entered a cave and disappeared into darkness. We checked our headlamps, climbed onto our float tubes, and drifted slowly down the river as we entered the mouth of the cave. The outside light of the world faded quickly, and we all began to realize just how inadequate our tiny headlamps were in a place that was completely absent of light.

As we floated through the cave, our guide explained the significance of this region of Belize. Large underground river systems flowed through the mountains, systems so complex that parts are still unmapped. By the dim light of our headlamps, we could barely make out the ledges on both sides of the cave as our guide described them. Some people grew uncomfortable as he pointed, relaying small tidbits about archeological finds, "We found human bones in here," and "We think people were sacrificed over there." His solemn words only served to amplify the eerie feel of the dark place, which shouldn't come as a surprise. For the ancient Mayans who lived in this part of the world, this was no mundane, ordinary river and cave system. It was intrinsically supernatural in essence and structure: this was an entrance to their underworld.

As we continued to float through the caves, our guide suggested we turn our lights off so we could float in the experience of pure darkness. It was too overwhelming for some; one member of our party began to cry softly. As sight faded, the other senses grew as the mind tried to process the experience of this eerie place. What was that your tube just brushed against under the water? It sure didn't feel normal. What just scraped against your arm? It didn't feel like a rock. Was that a dead branch that washed into the cave, or was it part of an ancient, sacrificial skeleton?

In some places the river was extremely shallow, and we could feel rocks brushing just underneath us. Then suddenly someone would end up in a slow-moving corner of the cave that was just a few feet away from the quick, shallow water. The water in these calm parts clearly had much more depth than the surrounding shallow areas. Our guide explained that these were the holes in the floor of the riverbed that run inexplicably deep and straight down into the earth. In one particular eddy, where my wife found herself stuck, the guide explained they had been unable to locate the bottom, not by human divers, and not even by the high-tech National Geographic research team that he guided a few years earlier. The scientists had even brought remote diving devices and cameras that could go far deeper than the human divers could go in that environment. We were entering the Mayan underworld in total darkness and becoming stuck in eddies that were essentially bottomless.

It was an intimidating and otherworldly experience. I understand why the Mayans viewed this place as a place with a supernatural aspect, as space where the connection between the earthly, human realm meets the path into the underworld, which led into the place of dead people and spirits. I think there were a few people with us that day who were convinced that they might end up joining those dead spirits during our journey along that mystical river.

Patterns in Underworld Thought

The concept of the subterranean region is common in religious thought, typically following the ancient pattern of the underworld being a place of the dead or of evil spirits, maybe including a lower deity or spirit assigned to watch over the dead souls. This is a relatively familiar pattern even to modern humans (after all, we tend to bury our dead underground). However, there are some variations in the particulars of how each culture interpreted and applied this pattern. For example, the Hopi Indians of the Third Mesa believed that the dead lived in a lower region,[31] but their world of the dead was a place of happiness, not of suffering. While the pattern is the same (the dead exist in the subterranean realm), it's important to note that one of the particulars (the situation of the dead) of the subterranean realm of Third Mesa Hopi Indians differs significantly from the particulars of the vast majority of subterranean religious patterns. The particulars of each religious symbol will always be at least a little different between religious expressions, but the overall pattern generally holds true regardless of those particulars.

The Aztecs, as shown in a poem about the greatness and importance of Tenochtitlan, described the earth as sitting on a single layer above the underworld—which had nine layers of its own.[32] Their mythology spoke of a psychopomp (a guide for the dead) named Xolotl who descended into their version of the underworld and aided in gathering the dead.[33]

Far away from the Americas, in a typical form of historical Asian shamanism, certain rituals and beliefs taught that the shaman's spirit left his body to travel to the underworld, which was a land of the dead and of evil spirits.[34] In some of these rituals, the shaman would fall to the ground and writhe in mock agony as he imitated being tortured by the demons belonging to the underground realm.

Greek mythology demonstrated the classical concept of the underworld as the place of the dead. A passage in a famous Greek play *Oresteia* revealed a human devotee asking the god Hermes to share his prayers with the spirits in the underworld.[35] The underground realm of the dead was prevalent in their stories, including the boatman that ferries people across the water to reach the dead souls.

Likewise, the Babylonians, eventual conquerors of Israel and fellow residents of the Middle East, believed in a hollow region underneath the surface of the earth, and they taught of an underworld realm of the dead.[36] The Sumerians wrote of an underworld with an evil demon named Asag.[37] This ancient concept was very widespread throughout ancient Near Eastern thought. The underworld was always a place of the dead, and it was located under the surface of the earth.

Moving to Christian times in Europe, we can see the same thought pattern. From the tenth to the fifteenth century CE, reports and rumors of satanic cults spread throughout Christendom. They all followed the same pattern: evil, abhorrent practices taking place in underground caves with evil spirits present.[38] Once again the pattern of being underground with evil spirits is demonstrated in these tales.

Underworld Patterns in the Bible

The Bible contains several examples of this type of thinking. For example, when Jacob thought that his son Joseph had been killed, he said, "Surely I will *go down to Sheol* [hell] in mourning for my son" (emphasis added, Genesis 37:35). Note that he had to travel *down* and it was associated with death and mourning. Hell is equated to the pattern of the underworld in this biblical story.

Another powerful example occurred much later during the Israelite's desert wanderings. In this terrifying tale, more than 250 rebellious leaders were swallowed up by the earth in a clear symbol (that was also very literal!) of descending to a lower realm of the dead.

But if the LORD brings about an entirely new thing and the *ground opens its mouth and swallows them up* with all that is theirs, and they *descend* alive into Sheol, then you will understand that these men have spurned the LORD. As he [Moses] finished speaking all these words, *the ground that was under them split open*; and *the earth opened its mouth and swallowed them up*, and their households, and all the men who belonged to Korah with their possessions. So they and all that belonged to them *went down alive to Sheol*; and the earth closed over them, and they perished from the midst of the assembly. All Israel who were around them fled at their outcry, for they said, '*The earth may swallow us up!* (emphasis added, Numbers 16:30-34).

These examples from the Old Testament demonstrate a thought pattern that teaches there is a lower realm that is a place for the dead. It is associated with being under the surface of the earth. It also demonstrates that it is a place for evil people to go who are at odds with God. Joseph and the rebellion of Korah are just two examples selected from many that are in the Old Testament.

We also find examples in the New Testament. Many centuries after Moses, Jesus confronted a swarm of demons who possessed a man. As they were about to be exorcised, they asked Jesus not to send them *into the abyss* (Luke 8:31, emphasis added). This would fulfill the pattern of being both underground and a place of evil spirits. Paul also refers to the abyss (Romans 8:7) as does John in his apocalyptic vision. "And he laid hold of the dragon, the serpent of old, who is the devil and Satan, and bound him for a thousand years; and he threw him into the abyss, and shut it and sealed it over him" (Revelation 20:2-3). The abyss is an underground area of evil spirits, punishment, and death. Clearly, the ancient pattern of the lower region holds true in the Bible, both in the Old and New Testaments.

The subterranean realm of the dead and evil spirits is one of the easiest ancient patterns to identify and understand. It persisted through most religions, and it shows up in Christian creed, famous paintings, and in Dante's famous writing. The concept should be easy for modern people to understand.

However, while it is important for us to understand the idea of the subterranean realm and its widespread presence in ancient cultures, of far greater significance to us is the concept of the sky and the realm of the heavens. We're going to leave the dark, dead underworld for now as we move on to look at the upper realm and visit the home of the divine.

CHAPTER 4:

Up in the Heavens

AS A CHILD GROWING UP, I found Greek myths to be fascinating and fun. I would go to the Puyallup library and check out stacks of books at a time (the librarians knew me and kept paper grocery bags around so I could carry all the books home easier). I devoured the books and read all the major Greek literature. I played video games based on Greek myths on my Commodore 128. My dad was a seminary student and we had Greek books in the house, which I tried to use to learn Greek on my own (unsuccessfully). I remember going to Greek tragedies put on at the Intiman Theater at the Seattle Center. The one Greek deity who really stood out was, of course, Zeus. He was the god of thunder who lived at the top of Mount Olympus. The Greek myths accounted for lightning storms by claiming Zeus cast lightning down from the heavens in a show of power or displeasure. It's just myth, of course, and it's not true, but it's a fun thing to read about. Living in the Pacific Northwest, we didn't really get much in the way of lightning and thunder, and what little we did receive wasn't frightening or a display of vast power, but I could guess at what the ancient Greeks experienced that formed the basis for their stories.

Chris and I experienced a powerful lightning event one night as we drove back to our home in Salt Lake City (during the one year we lived there). We were approaching the city from the west, and right when we hit the Salt Flats we encountered a thunderstorm the likes of which I hope to never experience again. Lightning struck all around us literally every few seconds the entire way home (nearly a two-hour journey). It didn't stop once we got back; it lasted through most of the night. The flashes filled our home like a strobe light, and the massive rumbling thunder simply would not stop. Our home shook, and I was a bit on the fearful side the entire time. The local news the next day estimated that over one thousand lightning strikes occurred in the city during the night (and that didn't count the ones we experienced as we drove in). Even for modern humans who understand why lightning strikes occur and what creates the massive roars of thunder, the experience was very unusual and intimidating, particularly for someone who grew up in an area that received only one or two very mild thunderstorms a year (at most). It's easy to understand how ancient people would have viewed a storm like that as a supernatural event originating with the deities who lived in the upper realm. Through my experience that night, I understood a bit more of the Greek mindset about the upper realm.

The Sky

It's easy for any one of us to spend time stargazing or watching the clouds in the sky and realize some sense of transcendence. We can see *through* the sky to whatever is beyond, and we can gain a sense of vastness, beauty, power, and wonder. As Eliade observed, the basic act of gazing at and thinking about the vast, infinite expanse of space was probably sufficient to induce religious-style thought in ancient people. It may even do the same for many modern humans today. Contemplating the incredible expanse of space or the sky reveals the finitude of humanity, while at the same time communicating the existence of something else:

something that is very real, yet, something people do not physically experience. We are constrained to our earthly realm although we think about the majesty of the vast, open spaces. If we attempt to comprehend the extent of space, our minds attempt to define something that dwarfs human existence by virtue of its extreme magnitude.[40]

This human perception of the upper sky realm probably contributed to the human perception of divine transcendence. Most belief systems claim there is something more than just the mundane, ordinary human existence we all know. That "something more" is powerful, real, and of a higher order of existence than mere humans. Geisler and Corduan point out that in whatever way people define it, it is worthy of worship, devotion, obedience, and sacrifice. To sum it up with one word, it is the Transcendent.[41] We ought to be able to understand this concept on some level since we encounter the Transcendent in our own personal faith or see it reflected in the religious behavior of others we know. As we perceive the sky, space, and stars to be above the realm of the earth and beyond human reach, they naturally reflect the nature of the transcendence: something higher and greater than mere humans or the human realm. Consistent with this line of thinking, most ancients considered the upper region to be the home of the divine, the place where many of the gods and other divine beings lived.

Examples of the Sky Realm in History

Early people's concepts of God (or gods) involved a sky epiphany.[42] They thought the divine, whoever that was to each society, lived in or was part of the upper, heavenly realm. Once again, this was a universal belief across societies.[43] Prehistoric cave art found throughout the European continent shows humans raising their arms *toward the heavens* in supplication and worship of the good gods or spirits.[44] Rock tracings found in Scandinavia and in ancient Irish cairns depict solar cults who worshipped a sky deity.[45] Some tribes in pre-agricultural Africa worshipped a supreme sky deity.[46]

Moving forward from ancient people, Native American tribes showed similar beliefs about a sky god. For example, the Iroquois word for "on high" virtually matches the name of their chief deity, indicating a clear connection between the two.[47] In pre-Shinto, pre-Buddhist Japan, various religious activities denote belief in a sky god.[48] In Mongolia, the Mongol name for their deity literally meant "sky."[49] You can't get clearer than that.

One well-known continuation of this belief comes from the Greeks. *The Odyssey of Homer* describes the supreme deity of their pantheon, Zeus, as a god who creates thunder from up in the heavens.[50] In Greek mythology, Zeus is the supreme deity of their pantheon of gods, and he is the sky god who throws lightning down toward the earth. People often viewed lightning as an act of the divine that reached from the god's home in the heavens down to the earthly realm.

The belief in the sky as the realm of the divine was also prevalent in the cultures that interacted with the people of the Bible. In Sumerian culture, the word for divinity actually referred directly to a sky epiphany.[51] In Assyria three of the major gods are clearly associated with the upper region: Adad is the god of storms,[52] the god Assur is represented by a solar disc,[53] and Anu is the god of the heavens.[54] An ancient seal found in the archives of the Bibliothèque Nationale shows two Babylonian worshippers stretching their hands up toward the sky realm worshiping the sun.[55] Egyptians worshipped Ra, the god whose emblem was the sun.[56] Some Persian art also demonstrates this concept. One scholar even noted that the design patterns on Persian carpets clearly laid out the upper realm as the home of the divine.[57] Even a brief sample of the list of ancient cultures that participated in this belief system would be extremely long,[58] and it would be redundant to list them all. For us it is sufficient to recognize people thought the transcendent divine lived apart from the human-inhabited realm, instead residing in the upper region associated with the sky or space realm.

Biblical Examples of Upper-Realm Patterns

As an example of biblical thinking with regard to the upper region, read the story of Elijah's duel with pagan worshippers as they debated whose deity was supreme. In this situation, God sent fire to the earth *from out of heaven*, which then consumed the sacrifice (1 Kings 18:38). This indicated that God was in the upper strata. This is similar to the Greek pattern of Zeus sending lightning from the heavens. It is interesting to note that it was a duel between worshippers of Baal and worshippers of the God of Israel. Both sides were expecting their deity to operate from the sky realm to consume the sacrifice, but only the God of Israel did so.

The prophet Isaiah described the personified concept of a sky epiphany when he wrote, "He [God] who sits above the circle of the earth" (Isaiah 40:22a), and he did it again when he wrote, "lift *up* your eyes *on high* and see who has created these stars" (Isaiah 40:26a, emphasis added). The prophet wrote of the power of God to strengthen his weakened followers by saying, "They will mount up with wings like eagles" (Isaiah 40:31b), which is clearly a continuation of the sky epiphany and the upper realm.

In the New Testament, when Jesus taught the disciples how to pray, he started with "Our Father *who is in heaven*" (Matthew 6:9, emphasis added). Later, when describing his final return to the earth, he said, "And then the sign of the Son of Man will *appear in the sky*, and then all the tribes of the earth will mourn, and they will see the Son of Man *coming on the clouds of the sky* with power and great glory" (Matthew 24:30, emphasis added). Clearly, the writers of the Bible thought of God in line with the cultural forms of a sky epiphany. Several passages also indicate that the angels spend time in heaven (for example, Job 1:6 and 2:1; Revelation 5).

The widespread religious thinking regarding God of the gods as existing in the upper realm of the sky is clear. Whether a devout follower of Baal in the ancient Near East, a prehistoric person living in a cave, or a New Testament author, all the religious patterns point to a deity that dwells above the realm of the earth.

CHAPTER 5:

Stuck in the Middle

I'VE NEVER BEEN DRIVEN TO push to the extremes of human habitation. I am, as you might surmise, more of a bookworm than an adventure-seeker. Humanity is generally confined to life on the surface of the earth, and I've been perfectly content to stay there. I would explore some subterranean regions in my youth as my family would explore lava tubes in both Oregon and Idaho, but that's about as deep as I would go. I've never been far above ten thousand feet in elevation (except in an airplane), and then only via roads, lifts, or hiking trails. My adventures have been limited by the aftereffects of a battle with cancer I had at age twenty-five, but to be honest, I probably would have limited myself anyway. I'm happy to live vicariously through the adventures of others in this regard.

I have a good friend who loves to dive, and he dives in extreme and unusual places. He and his wife have proudly dived off of all seven continents (yes, including Antarctica). They have dived in the chasm between continental plates in Iceland. They dive regularly by their home in the Puget Sound. But even the best divers are limited by how deep they can go due to pressure limitations of the human body. You can only go so far before your life is at risk. The extreme depths of the seas are much more difficult. Even remotely operated vehicles with no humans inside can struggle to get all the way down to the depths where humanity can never go.

Turning away from the depths and looking upward, my mom and stepdad were mountaineers. My stepdad climbed Mount Rainier (ironically, he summited about the time I was flying overhead on a trip home from Mexico). However, the altitude (over fourteen thousand feet) got to him and he summited while experiencing a case of altitude sickness, which caused disorientation and confusion. In time, it can progress to a pulmonary or cerebral edema and can be fatal. He was so ill he doesn't remember much about his accomplishment. He never returned to an altitude like that again. The heights were too much for his body to handle. I also spent many years working for a man who loved to climb mountains. I don't mean just any mountains; he loved to climb the *really* tall mountains in extreme locations (near the South Pole) or mountains over twenty thousand feet (Himalayas, South America, Alaska). While still part of the earth's surface, these mountains push into the early fringes of the sky realm, and the thin oxygen and extreme conditions make it very dangerous for humans. During one of his expeditions, the very worst thing imaginable occurred: a member of his climbing team lost his life. The extreme conditions were too much for him, and tragedy claimed him. Most humans were just not made to live for long in the reaches approaching the upper realm, and doing so always come with a risk.

Life always has risk no matter where you live. You cannot eliminate all risk, nor should you try to do so. My friends who push the limits have always returned safely, and I pray they always do. But I will be content to stay within the context of human existence: in the habitable realm on the surface of the earth: not too deep, and not too high.

The Inaccessible Heavens

After talking about the lower and upper realms in the previous chapters, we need to talk about the realm of humanity. As part of understanding the human realm, there is one specific aspect to the religious thought about the sky realm that is important to understand: no one can get there on his or her own. The sky is off limits to people, and it is beyond human ability to dominate, control, or subjugate the heavens (as people are able to do with the surface of the earth to a certain extent). We can live on the earth, but we can't live in the sky. For the most part, we generally choose where we want to go on the earth, but we lack the ability to do that in the heavenly realm. On the rare occasions we do this, we do it by transplanting the earthly atmosphere to the sky realm on a limited basis (think of an airplane or the International Space Station). The heavenly realms simply don't belong to us.

The Greek tale of Icarus (which is probably adapted from even earlier myths) is a fantastic example of humanity's inability to access the heavens. Icarus and his father constructed homemade wings in order to soar in the sky. Icarus grew too confident, soared too high, and soon he was too close to the sun. The closer he got to the heavenly realm, the more tentative and weak his wings became. Eventually they gave out, and he plummeted to his death.[59] He ignored his father's warnings, and he paid the ultimate price. Unlike Icarus, who attempted to exist in or near the heavenly realm using his own human power, we know of a human in the Bible that did enter the heavens. Elijah entered the heavenly realm because God took him there. He did not attempt to enter heaven by his own human power. He went to Heaven by the invitation and mechanism provided by God. "And it came about when the LORD was about to take up Elijah by a whirlwind to heaven . . . there appeared a chariot of fire and horses which separated the two of them [Elisha and Elijah]. And Elijah went up by a whirlwind to Heaven" (2 Kings 2:1a, 11b). There is a separation between the heavens and the human realm that God or the divine can bridge, but humans cannot. Continuing the theme of separation, Jewish tradition teaches that the construction of the tabernacle included a symbolic representation of the concept of humanity's inability to enter the sky realm. Josephus reported that when Moses separated the tabernacle into three distinct areas, he allowed people to enter the first two parts, which both represented the earth (the middle layer). However, he set apart the third area and did not allow people to enter it. That third area represented heaven. It was a clear, symbolic statement that heaven was God's realm and that people could not enter into it unbidden.[60]

Life on Earth

Science fiction is a great way for the human mind to explore concepts of living that escape the confines of our current reality. In those tales, we see people who reside in fantastic settings, such as in the expanse of outer space or perhaps deep in the underground of a post-apocalyptic world. For the most part, it's pure fantasy, although it's fun to think about and guess what the future could hold. Sure, we have a few space-faring pioneers who have spent time in orbit, and people have certainly made use of caves and tunnel systems as shelter, but for the most part, humanity lives *on the earth*. We don't really live among the stars, and we don't live underneath the tectonic plates. This reality is exactly how the ancients perceived their existence in the universe: humans live in the realm of the *earth*.

Scholars of the history of religion note that people widely embraced this *pattern* of the structure of the universe in ancient thinking,[61] although some of the *particulars* with regard to how the universe arrived at this specific structure vary in many mythologies. Regardless, it's easy to see how people arrived at this perception. Obviously, there is a vast sky region above the earth where birds, stars, and planets move over our heads. Below our feet, the earth seems deeper than we can dig, and creatures, smoke, steam, fire, and rivers emerge from under its surface. Some caves and tunnels lead deeper into the earth than modern humans can fully explore, and sometimes the ground beneath us shifts violently. Dangerous pools of super-heated, molten rock lay beneath us. Humans live in the middle, caught between the heavens and the lower region.

In this mode of thought, the middle region of humanity consists of the regular surface of the earth, some shallow, lived-in caves, and most easily habitable lower-mountain regions. While technically part of the earth, some people believed that deeper tunnel systems led into the lower realm, and sometimes they perceived upper mountain heights as being a meeting point between the upper realm and humanity's domain in the middle, if not belonging to the sky region entirely. But, for the most part, wherever people were able to live with moderate effort, they perceived it was part of the middle realm of existence.

At this point we should look at a chart that clarifies the details of how ancient cultures generally viewed the strata of existence. When considering the three realms, the chart should read as follows:

Heaven: God, Angels, Souls of the Righteous Dead

The Earth: Humans

Hell: Demons, Souls of the Wicked Dead

We find this perception of the structure of existence *all over* the ancient world, including examples found among people in Asia,[62] Malaysia,[63] Australia,[64] Africa,[65] South America,[66] Mesopotamian cultures,[67] Pacific Northwest Indians,[68] and many more. This concept was prevalent enough that someone could probably write an entire book simply by cataloging these examples. While the particulars of each culture's various scenarios are different, the pattern remains the same: humans are stuck in the middle. While angels may not actually live up in the clouds or in outer space, and while the dead and demons may not truly inhabit some open pocket near the earth's core, the concept of humanity living in between an upper, holy realm and a lower realm of death and evil remains applicable.

I've lived my life relatively close to sea level. Most of my life has been spent between 100 and 750 feet above sea level, with one year spent about forty-four hundred feet above sea level. I can take easy journeys up to ten thousand feet, but that's not true for everyone. My father-in-law, Gene, tried to go up to Silver Lake in Utah while visiting us, but his heart could only handle so much, and we stopped around six thousand feet. That was his limit. People who are born into or condition themselves can handle much more, but even then, they have limits.

Since ancient people could not enter heaven and commune with the Divine by the force of their own will or actions, they were essentially stuck in the middle realm with no way to experience the Divine directly. Experiencing the Divine was not as easy as walking next door to have a chat with your neighbor. Unless the Divine entered into the middle realm in some fashion, there was no opportunity for interaction. In order for humankind to experience the sacred, the Divine had to make a choice to enter into the middle realm of earth and humanity. The Divine had to *manifest* itself into our human reality of time and space on the earth. And this is exactly how ancient people viewed supernatural experiences: The Divine/sacred/transcendent entered into (manifested itself in) the mundane realm of human existence (the middle layer between the upper realm and the lower realm). Mircea Eliade researched religious patterns and codified this area of research, and the word he used to represent this concept is *hierophany*, which means "a manifestation of the sacred."[69] The unspoken implication in the definition is that the manifestation of the sacred occurs in the middle realm. In the academic fields of history of religions and comparative studies of religion, the concept of hierophany is one of the most critical, core ideas that a person must understand.

If it is true that the sacred does indeed manifest itself in the profane realm of mundane human existence (as all religions teach), then that manifestation is a very special and important event. Accordingly, the behavior of the ancient people demonstrates that they valued any manifestation of the sacred (any hierophany) very highly. Due to the importance they placed on such an event, we are going to take a close look at the significance of a hierophany and its role in ancient life.

CHAPTER 6:

Hierophany and Meaning

ON THE MORNING OF APRIL 1, 2001, Chris and I woke to the serenade of birds perched in the branches of the surrounding Schwarzwald. We readied ourselves for a long day of sightseeing that would take us many miles from one region of Germany to another. Before leaving the Black Forest around noon, we shopped for cuckoo clocks, visited the Triberg waterfall, and enjoyed the scenic roads winding between rivers and mountains. Finally turning to head east, we took small, back roads across the southern part of the country toward our final destination in Bavaria. The entire trip would take only a few hours if we followed the major autobahn routes, but we preferred to experience the quiet scenery and meandering roads. As we drove east, we took detours to visit some of the quaint villages and tall castles populating the region. The daylight hours passed quickly, and soon we realized the second half of our journey would continue in the dark of night. Since we decided to avoid the autobahn and instead use local country roads, there was little in the way of light or signs. Clouds covered the night sky so we received no benefit of stars or moonlight to help us see the surrounding terrain or distant landmarks. The tall peaks of the Alps were not visible, and the small, twisting roads and unmarked intersections did not match anything we found on our map—they were probably too small to be of consequence to most travelers. Needing to make progress and reach our destination, we made a series of guesses about our location and drove according to what we thought was the right route. It wasn't (it was April Fool's Day after all). Late into the night, we eventually stumbled across the small town of Nesselwang, and to our exhausted relief, we found a small hotel with an open room and quickly settled in for some much-needed sleep.

As we ate breakfast in the hotel the next morning, we tried to plan the new day's driving route. Nesselwang was just large enough to show up on our map, so we could finally figure out exactly where we were. This showed us just how wrong our "educated" guesses were the night before. We must have driven every small farm road approaching southwest Bavaria the night before, circling around and crossing roads heading in the wrong direction, even triggering a traffic camera in one tiny village, before finally finding a place to stop. After finishing breakfast and folding up the map, we stepped out of the hotel into the cool air and blue skies of a fresh Bavarian morning. Immediately we could see the majestic Alps rising to the south and east of us—the same Alps we wanted to use for orientation the night before but could not see due to darkness. Now we could guide ourselves using external data we did not have the previous evening: the reference points of Nesselwang and the Alps. Using those two points of reference, we were able to pinpoint our location, plot a course, and journey toward our destination.

Finding Direction

In the thought of the ancient people, the world of mere humans (the middle realm) is an ordinary world with no intrinsic supernatural quality to it. To use proper religious terminology, it is a *profane* existence. We might also use the word "mundane" to indicate it is an ordinary, regular existence as opposed to one that is intrinsically supernatural or sacred. At some point early in human history, people living in the profane, ordinary, middle realm probably encountered something they perceived as coming from another realm, perhaps the Divine appearing on the earth. These early encounters probably gave birth to the concept of the sacred.[70] Since hierophanies such as these were manifestations of something sacred in the middle of a profane existence, people valued them highly. Mircea Eliade believed these experiences were so important that they formed the basis for early religion.[71]

People have a natural tendency to look for external references to validate and guide their beliefs, lives, actions, and overall sense of meaning. This is similar to using landmarks as reference points to plot a journey. However, a purely profane world lacks external points of guidance (reference points from outside the profane realm). Finding good external guidance in a merely profane world is difficult. A person's own internal instinct may offer correct guidance, or that same instinct could be very wrong, much like my incorrect instincts were that dark night in southern Germany. Another individual's opinion and guidance equally could be right on target or way off base and misleading. Ultimately, any true, accurate sense of direction must come from reliable external landmarks or points of reference.

In a hypothetical reality that is entirely mundane with nothing divine or supernatural in any part of existence, there is nothing transcendent for people to observe or experience. This means there are no external (outside the immediate realm of existence) points of reference people can use to gauge meaning, receive guidance, or discern which values are most important. All value judgments and points of reference are arbitrary or subjective to each individual, which makes them of little or no value. In order to gain any accurate sense of direction or orientation, there must be something external (an outside point of reference) you can refer to and navigate by.

Consider the example of being lost at sea and floating in the middle of a calm ocean on a cloudy night with no survival gear. There are no currents, no stars, no moon, no sun, no compass, and no sign of land—*nothing at all.* Take a minute to picture yourself in this place and think about what the experience would be like. No wind blows, and no birds fly. The only thing you can see is water. You can't even tell if you've moved or if you're in the exact same spot as you were an hour earlier. Everywhere you look is featureless, calm water. You are truly and hopelessly lost.

There might be a few other lost sailors floating nearby, which might provide a false sense of security. However, if no one can see an external reference point, then everyone is still lost, despite the comfort of company. The group may genuinely believe they are floating off the coast of New Zealand within a few miles of the shore, *but their sincere belief and genuine agreement does not make it true.* They may actually be hundreds of miles from land and far from salvation. In reality, sailors need external reference points in order to figure out where they are as well as how to get to a particular location. Those reference points can be the magnetic north pole, the North Star, the paths of the sun and moon, sightings of land, sea currents, prevailing wind patterns, etc.

Like people lost at sea, humans require reference points for living in order to gauge any guides or meaning for life. Superior, external points of reference—such as manifestations of the divine—serve as a guide or authority when considering values, conduct for life, and how to determine truth. Attempting these meaningful activities without reference points is wholly ineffective. Even if two or more people without reference points agree on something subjective (like the sailors lost at sea), their agreement is meaningless since the lack of an external measure renders agreement just as meaningless as disagreement.

The same idea applies to values, meaning, morals, relationships, and more. The lyrics sung by Eva Briegel in "Seenot"[72] poignantly capture the feeling of this concept by using the metaphor of someone lost at sea. The protagonist in the song drifts aimlessly on a raft crying out for a sign, a point of reference, or a reason that provides significance in her life.[73]

In the early world, life without the Divine was similar to the experience of floating lost at sea. Then the occurrence of a hierophany revealed an absolute reality that stood in stark contrast to the undifferentiated subjectivity of their purely profane human existence.[74] For ancient societies, the revelation of sacred reality and higher existence could provide meaning and guidance for life. The first hierophany became a point of absolute reference for life: it was a guide where previously one did not exist.[75] This would be similar to the lost sailor finally spotting land in the distance and having a reference point for his sailing.

Variety in Hierophany

With this in mind, it's easy to understand why early religions centered themselves on hierophanies.[76] However, humankind is at the mercy of the divine: hierophanies only occur when something from another realm manifests itself in our middle realm. The sacred is not subject to the whim of the profane; an individual cannot force the divine. Due to their importance and humanity's inability to determine when and where they occurred, every society marked the locations of hierophany or remembered rituals that appeared to be associated with them.

The hierophanies showed great diversity between people and cultures, varying between simple, complex, holistic, cryptic, provoked, or obvious.[77] A single religious person likely experienced a large variety of hierophanies during his or her lifetime. For example, we see several people in the Bible who experience multiple hierophanies. Despite any differences between hierophanies, when something supernatural and out of the ordinary occurred, it indicated the presence of the sacred manifested in the middle realm as a hierophany. For example, think about the burning bush Moses encountered. Flames engulfed a bush on the mountaintop, but the fire did not consume the bush—a very odd occurrence indeed! Even stranger, a voice spoke to Moses from out of the burning bush. This was something that Moses did not normally encounter in his profane, ordinary existence. This event had an obvious supernatural aspect to it. It was a hierophany, and it indicated divine interaction with the profane realm. Other examples from the Bible include the tongues of fire on the day of Pentecost, the light from heaven Saul experienced on the road to Damascus, and the pillar of smoke and fire leading the Israelites in the wilderness. There is a plethora of examples in the scriptures.

However, some hierophanies were not quite as obvious. Occasionally, someone heard an unusual noise and thought it might be supernatural in origin, despite the lack of something visually impactful (a very odd noise without the visual clue of a burning bush). Perhaps an individual might perceive a natural event as having a supernatural aspect to it, something like a lightning bolt hitting a tree (normal) but not causing damage to the tree (seemingly unusual).[78] A particular location where someone experienced visions or apparitions was notable as well. For example, certain locations gained reputations as places of divine visitations, particularly mountaintops. Sometimes, people perceived an animal's unusual behavior as having a supernatural cause, hence the perception of a hierophany.[79] Think back to the story of Balaam's donkey for a time when an animal was the first to react unusually to a supernatural event. Balaam did not understand why he could not get the donkey to move. He tried and he tried. Eventually the donkey spoke and told him that an angel was blocking the path. The behavior of the donkey, its temporary ability to speak, and the presence of the angel are all indicators of a hierophany (Numbers 22:21-35).

The streak of a meteorite falling to the earth and the location of its earthly impact is another example of something people have perceived as having a spiritual association: the descending streak of light was indicative of the divine realm reaching down to the earth.[80] For example, the Kaaba's famous black stone, which is a cornerstone for Islam's holiest site, is reputed to be either a meteorite or more likely the glass created by the superheated impact of a meteorite.[81] According to the Hadith, it has been treated as a holy site since the pagan religions that long preceded Muhammed.[82] Today modern people view meteorite impacts as regular, scientifically understood events, but to the early people living in that area, it seemed as if something from the heavenly realm had descended to earth in that location.

Some people also thought that some natural features of the earth had hierophanic value,[83] particularly if the immediate geography was unique. Perhaps a unique stone formation or other geological feature would stand out as highly unusual and invite speculation as to the role of the supernatural in that place. Ultimately, the early inhabitants of the earth might perceive almost anything out of the ordinary or seemingly *phenomenal* as a hierophany, even though modern people often don't perceive things the same way.[84]

Whether ancient or modern, pagan or Christian, Hindu or Buddhist, the human desire for interaction with the Divine is universal. The hierophany provides this crucial point of connection between the believer and the Divine. It is the foundation of religious behavior and is central to our study moving forward.

CHAPTER 7:

Connection

SOMETIME IN 2011, THREE SENIOR pastors from various churches on the Enumclaw Plateau formed a local gathering of pastors, elders, theologians, and trusted confidants. They named it the "Spurgeon-Lewis Consortium." My senior pastor asked me to be a part of this select group that represented a variety of diverse religious backgrounds, traditions, and viewpoints: from Lutheran to Catholic, Calvinist to Open Theist, Pentecostal to non-Pentecostal, etc. These three pastors knew each other well and valued having close, trusted friends with whom they could share their lives, find people willing to listen, offer opinions, support each other, and relax among the rigors of ministry. Meeting once a week, the Spurgeon-Lewis Consortium introduced each of us to new, true friends who understood and supported each other as we walked through the difficulties of being flawed people doing God's work as best we could, while falling short more often than we would like. Sometimes we helped each other deal with issues of church business, such as keeping a positive attitude while former church members were attacking the pastor or church in the community. Sometimes Consortium members sought advice from other members who had excelled at performing a particular ministry before, such as Middle School Youth. Sometimes the conversations turned theological as we discussed the merits of meticulous sovereignty, open theism, and everything in between. Sometimes we just got together and laughed for three hours straight at the various stories and challenges of life. But at some points, life was too grim for laughter.

I remember sitting there as one pastor looked around at the Consortium with deep sadness, the usual gleam of joy gone from behind his eyes, and said, "I'm going to need to lean on you for the next several months." It was part plea and part resigned statement of reality: doctors had just diagnosed his wife of forty-nine years with cancer, and the prognosis appeared terminal. As his wife went through the ups and downs of treatment, as they went from signs of new hope to crushing reversals, and as she eventually passed into the presence of God, the Consortium provided a place where this pastor could let go and share his deepest thoughts and frustrations without fear of judgment. He knew the Consortium members would support him in person and in prayer without risk of us looking down on him.

It was that way for all of us. We all had struggles to share, and as our trust and connection to one another grew, we risked more and shared more. As our challenges grew deeper, our times of laughter and fellowship also grew richer. For me personally, the Consortium was a lifesaver. It was a place of honesty without judgment, but still a place where other men would reach into my life with sage advice, correction, and friendship. On several occasions, we all echoed the thought that our weekly time of connection was perhaps the best and most important time of the week. It was a place where men in ministry received the nurturing connection we so often provided for others without the fear of backlash or broken confidence. The group not only fostered a healthy connection to other people in ministry, it strengthened us in our Christian walk. We knew we were unlikely to recreate this sort of reliable connection elsewhere, and it seemed like a divine blessing to have the right individuals helping one another face difficult life circumstances. Individually and collectively, we sought to preserve and perpetuate this weekly time of connection that was so impactful in our lives. Authentic, reliable points of connection can play an important role in maintaining balance, staying emotionally and spiritually healthy, and keeping on track in our lives. Human beings were made for connection: with each other and with God.

Axis Mundi: The Sacred Connection between Heaven and Earth

Despite the variety and differences between the hierophanies experienced by each culture, every single hierophany indicated a crossover point between at least two of the three strata (heaven, earth, underworld). Most of the time the hierophany indicated that something from the upper plane (the heavens) broke through into the middle plane where humans lived. When that hierophany occurred, the people noted the particular geographic location where it occurred. They did this because they believed the Sacred either created this as a brand-new entry point or used a pre-existing break between planes to enter into the profane realm and manifest itself.[85] They seemed to think that this break in the boundary between the realms could be a permanent break (or at least long-lasting), which meant *it was likely that the divine would manifest in this specific location again* at some point in the future. As a result, people often considered these specific locations to be intrinsically sacred.

The cultures surrounding the people of the scriptures thought this was especially true: once the presence of the sacred had consecrated a particular location by its manifestation, it was likely to return to that location again in the future.[86] This was very important to them, because once people knew there was a break between planes that allowed the sacred to manifest itself again in the future, they knew a location where they could, theoretically, connect with the sacred and commune with the divine.[87]

Think back to the previous chapter. Since the heavens, where the divine dwells, are inaccessible to humankind, and since the presence and absolute reality of the sacred divine is vital for human orientation and guidance, people need a way to connect with the divine in order to obtain meaning and reference. Using the break between planes, the hierophany effectively establishes a vertical connection between realms called an *axis mundi*.[88] It connects the realms (heaven, earth, and the underworld) and potentially allows for communication and interaction between the three strata. For people who acknowledge the legitimacy of a particular hierophany, they acknowledge a connection that goes either upward from the human plane (toward heaven), downward from the human plane (toward the underworld), or into both.[89] The upward connection to the heavens is of greater universal concern for religious behavior, although sometimes the downward connection contained significant value as well, as it did in some shamanistic cultures.[90] The diagram below shows a basic representation of the concept of sacred connection between the strata of existence.

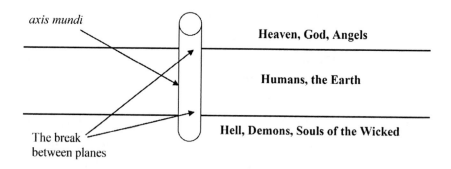

Axis Mundi as a Center

As a place where a hierophany enabled the connection between the sacred and the profane (and hence believers gained existential reference and meaning), any axis mundi was extremely important. Since people thought the break between planes would continue in some form over time, it was important to mark the location of the axis mundi for successive generations to come. That location could be of central religious value for as long as that particular society existed. In addition, people often knew of multiple axis mundi and marked them all. After all, the divine was free to manifest itself in any form or place as often as it wished.[91] One particular hierophany, which implied the presence of an axis mundi, did not replace or devalue any other—it simply provided people with an additional point of connection with the divine. Despite the multiplicity of connections, any hierophanically revealed axis mundi were important enough to be a point of focus, a *center*, whereby they maintained the valuable connection with the divine.[92]

The center implied by a hierophanically revealed axis mundi was where absolute, objective, sacred reality entered the subjective, profane, ordinary world of ancient humans. This revelation of a fixed reality provided people with a foundation to understand the essence, nature, and purpose of being (an ontological foundation).[93] Since it was a reference point for living and meaning, life essentially revolved around this point; it became a *center*.[94] A center like this does not always imply a geographic center, such as the geometric center point of a circle or the centermost area of a village (although on occasions they were). Sometimes they were ideological centers—points of grounding for theories and value propositions about all aspects of life: social, religious, philosophical, and so on—this is something religion provides for people. Once a person experienced the absolute, transcendent sacred, there was no other way to live than being connected to the divine (in whatever form people perceived it).[95]

The importance of ideological centers helps us understand why symbolism of the center is found everywhere in ancient societies, and for the most part it also explains religious behavior relating to sacred space.[96] Humanity's ongoing desire for connection with the divine drove people to create a variety of symbols, myths, and rituals by which they could recognize, remember, and invoke the use of the centers (axis mundi). One ancient example of this is the secretive Assyrian rituals that made use of a symbolic object known as the Mouth-and-Tongue. This symbol represented the vertical axis that took prayers from the humans in the earthly realm up to Ishtar, a goddess, who then in turn took prayers further up in the heavens to the greater gods. This object was the axis mundi, the center point of sacred connection, for the Assyrians who participated in these rituals. It represented the only way by which someone could communicate with the gods and hope to change his or her personal fate.[97] Like the Assyrian object that represented a way to communicate with the divine, all ancient axis mundi became the critical points of sacred connection for ancient people, and therefore each one was a central part of life.

Human Representation of a Center

People established a variety of ways to recognize these all-important centers. Some of the symbols and items used to represent the axis mundi were naturally occurring, vertically oriented natural features, such as trees or tall stones, and they happened to be located at the place where something supernatural occurred. In the third tablet of the Baal Cycle from Ugarit, Baal speaks in terms that we recognize as an archetypical representation of an axis mundi:

> For a message I have, and I will tell you.
> A word, and I will recount to you,
> Word of tree and whisper of stone,
> Converse of Heaven and Earth...[98]

Note that Baal starts by indicating he desires communication (a form of connection). Next, he speaks of tree and stone, which we will soon see are common symbols of axis mundi and central divine connection. In the last line, he specifies the conversational connection between the upper and middle realms. The time frame of this tablet fragment roughly corresponds to the stories of Gideon as recounted in the book of Judges (approximately the twelfth century BCE), but the tablet reflects stories and traditions that go back much earlier.

A specific tree-like example comes from the story of Moses. The burning bush on the mountaintop was just an ordinary bush on an ordinary mountain up until the point that God spoke to Moses in that location. At that point, the bush on the mountain became a point of a very real connection with God. It became a place where the divine manifested and interacted with (connected to) the mundane.

But not every mountain, tree, or tall stone was holy. For every axis mundi associated with a specific natural feature, many more of the same types of features were normal and ordinary. However, for obvious reasons, anything that had a vertical aspect to it invited hierophanic thought quite naturally. After all, something that appeared to stretch from the earth into the heavens provided a visual cue for the metaphysical concept of the axis mundi, and if a seemingly supernatural event occurred in that location, the association of the vertically oriented object with a hierophany and axis mundi occurred naturally to the human mind. Accordingly, we can find a huge variety of trees and mountains that people considered to be axis mundi.[99] The Mayans, for example, viewed the caves in mountains as particularly holy places of connection, which contained meaning for life and a focal point for rituals, since a mountain reached up toward the sky realm and the cave stretched downward toward the underworld. Hence, the Mayan ascription of value to the mountain caves followed the exact form of an axis mundi/center that made a connection for humans between the upper and lower realms.[100]

Besides the naturally occurring geographic features that were hierophanically consecrated and thought to be axis mundi, some human-made objects received the same treatment. For example, if a hierophany occurred in the middle of a flat area, sometimes an ancient society created something to commemorate and represent the axis mundi. Due to the importance of the center implied by the hierophany, they wanted to mark the location as sacred despite the lack of a natural vertical feature. People often used items like poles or vertically oriented stones to mark this sacred space.

In some examples, the use of rituals could also consecrate a site or object as a center symbol. The famous ball courts found in Aztec ruins—which served as a focal point for some spiritually related activities—contained a symbol of the center in the middle of each court.[101] This symbol was not mere decoration. It was acknowledgment of sacred space and the importance of divine connection.

At other times, both natural and human-made features combined into a single representation of an axis mundi. In recent times in India, the "anthill" rituals made use of termite mounds rising up out of the earth as axis mundi. The people believed the ventilation shafts of the mound, which stretched down into the earth, represented a break or point of connection between the lower realm of dead ancestors and the earthly realm of living humans. Since they recognized this axis mundi as a point of connection between the realms, they would often stick a pole in the top of the mound that stretched upward toward the heavens, and it would have a solar disc on the top that explicitly represented the heavenly realm. At this point, the modification to the termite mound explicitly showed connection between all three realms. This specific representation of the axis mundi made use of both natural and human-made elements.[102]

In the case of created symbols, we must realize that nothing ordinary people created in this regard contained any intrinsic, divine value on its own—*none whatsoever.* Rather, the divine had already manifested and established a metaphysical axis mundi irrespective of human activity, recognition, or marking of location. The subsequent human action was just a profane representation and reminder of the sacredness that already existed in that place. The actual value of a symbolic object was that it *pointed to that which is truly sacred.*[103] Of course, it was then very easy for humans to ascribe extra value to such a religious object because of the object's perceived participation in this transcendent reality.[104] It was probably the blurring of this differentiation between the object itself and the sacred it represented that allowed idolatry to creep into religion.

As we move into the next chapters, we're going to take some time to look closely at the various items, locations, and objects people consecrated as spiritual centers and axis mundi in history. Some of them will be familiar to you as sacred sites, some will be completely strange, and still others will be objects you're familiar with, but you may never have realized their significance. Nonetheless, to the people who made use of them, they all represented an axis mundi, and therefore they were centers for living. Above all, they represented the critical, necessary point of sacred connection that was so vital for life.

CHAPTER 8:

Stones

DURING THE SPRING OF 2004, Chris and I finally visited my ancestral home of Odell, which lies along the River Great Ouse approximately eight miles northwest of Bedford in the United Kingdom. Since I grew up hearing great stories about the village (some of which might have been true), visiting Odell was the main reason for our UK vacation. Besides visiting All Saint's Church, which the villagers founded in 1220 and completed during the fifteenth century, the highlight for us was having lunch at The Bell—pretty much the only place in town to grab a bite. While we were there, we happened to see Jon at the pub, who was our email contact in the village and ran the village website. While enjoying our chance meeting with Jon, he was surprised in turn to see Rev. David, the former vicar of All Saint's Church who served with distinction many years prior. Rev. David had just stopped by town to have lunch at The Bell, and it led to a great reunion and fantastic conversation, including Rev. David teaching me the proper way to pronounce "Odell," which also means I learned the proper way to pronounce the first half of my last name (turns out it rhymes with "yodel"). It was another object lesson in the importance of context and knowledge! The visit surpassed our expectations, and it was by far the highlight of our vacation. However, since we were already in the UK, we took the opportunity to visit some other fascinating places as well. During one of these side trips, we journeyed into the countryside and ended up at a very tiny village in the middle of farms and fields. This small hamlet is special because it is entirely contained within the boundaries of the world's largest known henge[105] enclosure.[106] In older times, the entire small village stood within the boundaries of the ancient stone circle. Talk about living in relation to the center—this village was literally there inside of it. Though the Romans ravaged much of the stones centuries earlier for building materials, several tall standing stones (many weighing more than a ton) still sat in wide circle around us while the remnants of a long avenue of standing stones stretched off into the distance.

Stonehenge may be the most famous preserved ancient henge, but is has nothing on the sheer size and feel of the Avebury circle. We had been to Stonehenge previously, and of course, we loved it. But for the two of us, Avebury held a greater sense of past grandeur and incredible human effort. The circle was enormous—estimates put it at 1,089 feet across—and its stone avenue stretched out even farther. There were almost one hundred stones used in just the outer circle at Avebury with many more used throughout the rest of the monument, and the nearest known place to harvest the type of stone the ancient people used is more than two miles away! The human effort required to quarry, transport, and erect the Avebury circle is difficult to comprehend.

We spent the afternoon wandering lazily among the stones while herds of fluffy, white sheep grazed in the stone-covered fields, with several lambs napping up against the stones in the warmth of the spring sun. The innocent, soft sheep stood out in contrast to the tall, hard stones that towered above them. Perhaps the scene on that day was similar to what it would have been thousands of years earlier, except for the tourists.

Megalithic Patterns

Sacred sites centered around standing stones are common throughout the world. Easter Island and Stonehenge may be the two most recognizable ancient megalithic[107] sites among thousands. The particular uses of megalithic sacred sites often varied from one group to another, and modern scholars still debate how various cultures used standing stones in each specific situation. For example, people used some for calendrical and astronomical purposes; they used others for fertility rites; and many remain a mystery. However different the particulars of each site may be, there is a basic, underlying pattern that spans culture and time: the standing stone (or stones) represents an axis mundi. It marks a location that is a place of divine presence and communication, which indicates an ongoing break between realms. It marks a sacred center. In his study of the core religious experience, Otto correctly noted that the motive behind people's establishment of standing stones was probably to remember and preserve a place of divine presence (a hierophany). It didn't matter if it was a single standing stone or a large circle of stones; the basic pattern was the same.[108]

We will look at three types of religious megaliths: natural stones, single standing stones, and stone circles. As we progress through these examples, remember that all religious experiences involving them had the same mythical-symbolic pattern at its core: hierophany and axis mundi. The standing stone represented a vertical connection between heaven, earth, and hell. The bottom of the stone rested under the surface of the earth (hell), passed through the zone of humankind (earth), and reached up along the vertical axis into the sky (heaven).[109] They were all sacred centers.

Let's start with a naturally occurring standing stone. Humans did not shape or move these megalithic axis mundi. Rather, people discovered these vertically oriented stones in nature. There are many reasons why someone may have considered a natural stone feature as spiritually significant. The standing stone may simply have struck a subconscious spiritual chord with an observer, or someone may have perceived a vertically oriented stone as the site of a hierophany if there was something noticeably out of the ordinary and unusual about it. As mentioned previously, someone might have observed a consecrating hierophany in the form of a strange sound, a flash of light, or an odd sensation experienced by a person standing near or touching the stone. It is also conceivable that a stone with a visually striking nature relative to its surroundings would have been enough to convince an ancient person of its transcendental and supernatural value. While we may not know why they considered it as such, the Semang pygmies of Malaysia considered at least one naturally occurring stone feature as sacred. They described *Batu-Ribn* as a gigantic, naturally occurring stone that was the center of their world. In demonstrating the pattern of connection between realms, they thought hell lay beneath the stone, and a tree stretched up toward the heavens from its top.[110]

Sometimes a hierophany occurred in a place that did not have a physical, vertically oriented counterpart in the immediate vicinity. In a situation like this, the ancient people could erect a megalith created from their own efforts. However, the simple act of erecting a human-made stone did not make the stone itself sacred. People already considered the site sacred due to the manifestation of the divine, and the stone simply marked the pre-existing sacred site. Besides marking the site of unprovoked hierophanies, sometimes people erected stones to commemorate a place where they attempted to invoke the divine as part of a ritual. Some examples might include invoking the divine to witness a contract, treaty, or some other occasion requiring divine authority and power, such as the story of Jacob and Laban detailed later in this chapter. There are many examples of single standing stones ancient people used for religious purposes, including hundreds of megalithic monuments just in Europe alone, examples of which include various columns found all over the European continent. For example, in 1904 a Jupiter Column was unearthed in Mainz, Germany. It had been smashed into more than two thousand pieces, likely by Christians who came along later and decided to destroy the object of false worship. Reconstruction estimates placed it at thirty feet tall, and they found an inscription dedicating the pillar to the god Jupiter.[111]

Likewise, a collection of stone pillars arranged in a circle uses the same basic megalithic pattern as a single stone pillar by itself. While a stone circle obviously has many more stones than the single stone pillar by itself, people still oriented them vertically, and they symbolize the potential of an ongoing hierophany and the presence of an axis mundi. Furthermore, the geometric nature of a circle also communicates the concept of a center where the connection between the realms can exist. With regard to more than five hundred stone circles dispersed throughout Europe, Souden noted that all stone circles contain vital meaning, and they all reference the heavenly realm (again pointing to an axis mundi connecting heaven and earth).[112] Stone circles may be associated primarily with Europe, but ancient stone circles have been found in places as varied as Wyoming, Japan, and Egypt.[113] All megalithic axis mundi, whether natural or hewn by humans, single or in a circle, indicated a point of sacred connection that local cultures used in their efforts to live in constant relation to the central divine.

Why Stone?

There is one particularly curious aspect of megalithic centers that we should examine: the decision of the ancient people to use stone. When human effort was required to create something to commemorate the hierophany and mark the place of an implied axis mundi, why did the ancient people use something as monumentally difficult to work with as stone? It was heavy, they had to quarry it, and oftentimes the source material was located far away from the sacred site. Working with giant blocks of stone was tremendously difficult, and it is still a challenge for modern people who have highly developed engineering skills, tools, and large machinery to do the heavy lifting. For the ancient people, using dirt, wood, or another substance would have been easier—anything but stone! While some societies did indeed use wood from time to time (wood had its own special aspect and function we will examine later), the multitude of standing stones, many of which stood among heavily forested regions or far from local quarries, cries out for an explanation.

Let's return to Stonehenge and look at the massive human effort required to build it. The stones the creators used are of a particularly hard variety, and people had to cut and shape the base stone using ancient methods and tools. Then they had to transport these humongous stones more than twenty miles to their current location. Then they had to raise some of the flat top-stones (lintels) approximately twenty-six feet into the air, and they joined them via carefully carved, matching features that fit together with surprising precision.[114] They accomplished all this without the benefit of our modern engineering techniques, vehicles for heavy lifting and transport, or power tools. Consider that Stonehenge is just one circle out of hundreds. People all over the world went to tremendous lengths to use what might have been the most difficult material possible for their symbolic centers. So why did they do it?

The answer lies in the human experience and perception of stone. For the ancient person, wood decayed, dirt eroded, and humans died; yet, stone remained seemingly unchanged. Stone is hard; it retains its shape and form over time (generally speaking). A stone represented strength and permanence in an ever-changing world, and in this regard, it resembled the absolute, permanent sacred transcending the ceaseless relativity of profane human existence. Unlike the other features of nature, when humans experienced stone, they experienced an absolute mode of existence that easily called to mind the qualities of the divine.[115]

A visit to the southwest area of the United States provides a great experiential demonstration of this concept. Yes, we know that stone does indeed change (via tectonic and erosive forces over countless years), but for the most part, the great stone features don't change notably within our lifetime, or even within several generations. If you've been fortunate enough to visit locations like the Grand Canyon, Arches, Bryce, and Zion, then you've encountered some natural stone features that are truly incredible and seemingly permanent. Each person experiences the massive, absolute stone features of these locations a little bit differently, but they are always astonishing and awe-inspiring to behold. I think they are all wonderful, but personally, I find that looking up from the bottom of the tall, abrupt canyons of Zion to be an experience that makes me feel small, finite, and subjective by comparison. It "puts me in my place" so to speak. The experience of standing at the top of the south rim of the Grand Canyon and contemplating the absolute sense of vastness generated by that experience generated a similar feeling for my wife. My sister, Kristina, experienced the Canyonlands in southern Utah in much the same way. Stone features feel permanent and powerful, and we seem very fragile and temporary in comparison.

By using stone for their centers (axis mundi), the ancient cultures made a clear declaration that a hierophany revealed the absolute (the Divine) to the finite and temporary (humans). Stone is hard, unchanging, and permanent, so it represents the reference point of a hierophany very well.[116] The difficultly in working with a medium such as stone was insignificant compared to the need to create an accurate, existential, persistent expression of the sacred center. This should further reinforce that the axis mundi was the vital reference for orientation in living. That is, the axis mundi became the centerpiece of living for ancient humans. These standing stones or stone circles were not necessarily a geometric center (as in people constructing their dwellings in concentric circles around a standing stone), but they were an ideological, spiritual, and moral center.[117] Life gained meaning and direction when lived relative to the absolute divine that the stones represented.

Standing Stones in Scripture

One only needs a general knowledge of scripture to understand that many practices associated today with neo-paganism, such as the specific worship and rituals conducted at standing stones, is not part of how a Christian is to conduct oneself before God. We worship the Triune God, not a stone. If someone reads the stories told in both the scriptures and history in general, it's clear that use of standing stones was a common pagan practice described and condemned in the Old Testament. However, in what appears to be a contradiction, some of the Bible's heroes also used symbolic stones, with God personally instructing the leaders of Israel in the establishment of these symbolic stones on at least one occasion. Similarly, the prophets continually decried pagan practices such as the veneration of and worship at high hills (see Jeremiah 2:20b for an example). However, the Psalmist also exhorted people to "Exalt the LORD our God and worship at *His holy hill*" (Psalm 99:9, emphasis added). The Christian scriptures, both the Old and New Testaments, are *filled* with ancient symbols, myths, and rituals, many of which are even taught and commanded by God in stark contrast to the corresponding condemnation of similar pagan practices. There is such an abundance of these examples in scripture that it would easily be a lifetime's work to fully identify, catalogue, and explain the intricacies of these symbols, myths, and rituals. As they are part of the Bible, which gives us God's divine revelation for humanity and His plea for people to accept His free, unearned gift of redemption, we should carefully examine and understand these seeming contradictions.

The ancient people of Britain, Malaysia, or Easter Island weren't the only people who used standing stones for religious purposes. We also see many examples of megalithic centers in the Bible. Let's start by looking at a couple of stories from the Book of Joshua.

As you may remember, Moses led the Israelites through the desert lands for about forty years after their escape from Egypt. After their long wilderness wandering, they were finally ready to enter into the Promised Land. After Moses died, Joshua led the people across the Jordan River and into the Promised Land. As part of the crossing, *God instructed* Joshua to make use of twelve symbolic stones. After they crossed, Joshua told his people to set up these stones as a witness to the significant event, saying, "Let this [the stones] be a sign among you" (Joshua 4:6a). A few verses later Joshua explained the purpose of the stones in more detail:

> Those twelve stones which they had taken from the Jordan, Joshua set up at Gilgal. He said to the sons of Israel, "When your children ask their fathers in time to come, saying 'What are these stones?' then you shall inform your children, saying, 'Israel crossed this Jordan on dry ground.' For the LORD your God dried up the waters of the Jordan before you until you had crossed, just as the LORD your God had done to the Red Sea, which He dried up before us until we had crossed; that all the peoples of the earth may know that the hand of the LORD is mighty, so that you may fear the LORD your God forever" (Joshua 4:20-24).

This is a great example of the symbolic use of a stone. God commanded Joshua to use these stones for His divine purpose. Joshua then commanded the people to set up the stones as something that symbolically pointed to God and to His connection with His people and His intervention in their lives. The stones themselves were not holy—only God is holy—but God used them to accomplish His will and to be a reminder to the Israelites of God's presence among His people and His involvement in their lives. That's exactly what a good symbolic center does.

Later on, Joshua again used stone as an example of the absolute nature of the sacred and its value in human living. He erected a stone as a symbol representing a divine witness. After all, God is an ideal witness; He is absolute and unchanging. What better way to represent His witnessing presence than with a megalithic axis mundi?

> And Joshua wrote these words in the book of the law of God; and he took a large stone and set it up there under the oak that was by the sanctuary of the Lord. Joshua said to all the people, "Behold, this stone shall be for a witness against us, for it has heard all the words of the Lord which He spoke to us; thus it shall be for a witness against you, so that you do not deny your God" (Joshua 24:26-27).

This wasn't the first time that someone in the Bible used a standing stone in this particular fashion. Several generations earlier Jacob did the very same thing when dealing with Laban. "'So now come, let us make a covenant, you and I, and let it be a witness between you and me.' Then Jacob took a stone and set it up as a pillar" (Genesis 31:44-45). When Jacob invoked God as a divine witness between two mortals, he took a naturally occurring stone and stood it up on end in the fashion of an axis mundi. This was no coincidence; Jacob was no stranger to the concept of an axis mundi. In fact, an earlier story from his life provides an explicit example of a hierophany, an axis mundi, and a center—sacred connection in its entirety—and a standing stone represents all of these concepts. This story occurs in Genesis chapter 28, which picks up after he has left the home of his father and is beginning a journey to establish his own life.

> He had a dream, and behold, a ladder was set on the earth with its top reaching to heaven; and behold, the angels of God were ascending and descending on it. And behold, the LORD stood above it and said, "I am the LORD, the God of your father Abraham and the God of Isaac;

the land on which you lie, I will give it to you and to your descendants. Your descendants will also be like the dust of the earth, and you will spread out to the west and to the east and to the north and to the south; and in you and in your descendants shall all the families of the earth be blessed. Behold, I am with you and will keep you wherever you go, and will bring you back to this land; for I will not leave you until I have done what I have promised you." Then Jacob awoke from his sleep and said, "Surely the LORD is in this place, and I did not know it." He was afraid and said, "How awesome is this place! This is none other than the house of God, and this is the gate of heaven." So Jacob rose early in the morning, and took the stone that he had put under his head and set it up as a pillar and poured oil on its top. He called the name of that place Bethel; however, previously the name of the city had been Luz. Then Jacob made a vow, saying, "If God will be with me and will keep me on this journey that I take, and will give me food to eat and garments to wear, and I return to my father's house in safety, then the LORD will be my God. This stone, which I have set up as a pillar, will be God's house, and of all that You give me I will surely give a tenth to You" (Genesis 28:12-22).

There is a lot packed into this section of verses. We're going to take it apart piece by piece and look at each part in detail. First, from the very beginning, the concept of an axis mundi is laid out in clear fashion—maybe one of the most explicit forms of an axis mundi from that time in history. Let's look at it again: "a *ladder was set on the earth with its top reaching to heaven*; and behold, the angels of God were *ascending and descending* on it" (emphasis mine). We clearly have the division between the realms of heaven and earth, and the ladder is the point of connection between the two realms. The story emphasizes the concept of the axis mundi by the angel's use of the ladder, which is the means to break through between the planes and travel down to the human realm (and back up again). As if to further emphasize the location of the divine and the concept of the axis mundi as coming from God, it says, "And behold, the LORD stood above it [the ladder]." Later, the LORD emphasized his presence with Jacob when he said, "I am with you and will keep you wherever you go." This is as precise an example of sacred connection as can be given.

Jacob spoke clearly about the consecrating presence of God when he cried out, "Surely the LORD is in this place, and I did not know it." He went on to say, "This is none other than the house of God, and this is the gate of heaven." Jacob knew that the hierophany specifically implied the presence of the divine (the presence of God), and he acknowledged that the break between heaven and earth had been established (persistently) in that location when he said, "this is the gate of heaven."

In recognition of this, Jacob set up a stone as a pillar. Note that Jacob moved the stone into a vertical position; it was not vertically oriented to begin with. He witnessed the axis mundi in his dream, and then he changed the orientation of the stone as an imitation of the vertical connection he saw. Then he poured oil on the stone, which is a human ritual recognizing divine consecration. The stone was already hierophanically consecrated by the presence of the divine, but Jacob went a step further. By anointing it with oil, he was imitating the divine hierophanic consecration, and in doing so, he recognized that while the stone was part of mundane, physical existence, it also pointed to the absolute, transcendent nature of the divine. The stone itself was not holy, but the presence of God is holy, and by anointing it, he recognized that the stone participated with sacred reality and pointed to God. Going further, he named the place Bethel (Beth-El), which literally means "house of God."

After that point, God began to occupy a place of central importance in Jacob's life. He talked about God being the source of his sustenance, clothing, and safety. He went even further when he referred to "all that you give me," and promised to give a tenth of it back to God. This story not only provides us with a fantastic biblical example of an axis mundi, it also shows the central role it played in human life. The stone Jacob set up, which pointed to God, represented a center for his life.

The Bible also provides other examples of the absolute, permanent nature of the divine as communicated by the use of stone in representing centers. The Song of Moses found in Deuteronomy 32, calls God "the Rock" on five separate occasions. The symbolic expression of God as the Rock culminates with a comparison between the pagan deities and the true God of Israel: "Indeed their rock is not like our Rock" (Deuteronomy 32:31a). An attentive reader will find this concept communicated throughout the scriptures. In Isaiah, for example, we can read, "Trust in the LORD forever, for in GOD the LORD, we have an everlasting Rock" (Isaiah 26:4), and, "Is there any God besides Me, or is there any other Rock?" (Isaiah 44:8). You may recall the Christian hymn "Rock of Ages," which manifests this type of thinking.

It is important that we take the opportunity re-emphasize something we cannot lose sight of: the stones described in the passages above contained *zero* intrinsic worth or value beyond that of any other stone. They were not holy in and of themselves. They were not items for people to worship. Certainly, worship of God probably did occur at locations like these, but true worship is always directed toward God and God alone, not toward an object He created. Paul wrote in Romans that part of people's sin is that they confuse the divinity of God with created things that might point to His divinity (Romans 1:22-25). It might be easy for those of us living today to understand this concept, but it was more difficult at times for the ancient people of the Bible. They struggled constantly with the difference between a sign (a representation) of the presence of God and with the nature and presence of true divinity itself. While the objects they used to represent and commemorate the axis mundi were simply mundane objects, sometimes they fell into the trap of thinking that the objects themselves contained some measure of divinity or that they were worthy of worship.[118] This is probably part of why the Ten Commandments state, "You shall not make for yourself an idol" (Exodus 20:4a) and "You shall not worship or serve them" (Exodus 20:5a). The bottom line is that we worship and serve God alone. We do not direct our worship to anyone or anything else. While we probably all have a cross (or several) in prominent locations in our churches, and while many churches and cathedrals also have a representation of Christ on the cross, we are never to worship the cross or the image of Christ. These objects simply serve as reminders that point to the true divine. Likewise, the examples of standing stones you just read about from the Bible were not holy themselves. Their authentic purpose was to remind people of the absolute, unchanging nature of the God who interacts with us, despite our mundane, sinful lives.

CHAPTER 9:

Mountains

I SEEM TO HAVE BEEN born with a particular fondness for mountains, so when I travel I find myself appreciating the special, unique qualities of the world's spectacular ranges. For me they are the greatest natural beauty God put upon the earth, and I feel rested and recharged in their presence. When we were deciding where to buy our first house, we only considered two communities in our area: North Bend and Enumclaw. Both are nestled up against the foothills of the Cascade Range, and they offer spectacular mountain views. It's my own personal preference, and I know they don't affect everyone in the same way. While my dad also loves mountains and took me to many ranges during summer breaks from school, he's really in love with the ocean. He loves to spend time along the Oregon coast and watch the waves break against the rocks or walk along its sandy beaches as the water sweeps up onto the gentle shore. By contrast, my father-in-law, Gene, loved the more arid regions of the American Southwest; to him there was no place more beautiful than the deserts of Arizona. He found the hills outside of Phoenix to be visually entrancing, and taking in those vistas recharged him. But for me, there's no place I'd rather be more than in the mountains. My earliest memories involve these stone-and-earth behemoths: walking on mountain trails, following mountain streams, swimming in mountain lakes, and even the eruption of Mt. St. Helens during my childhood in 1980. I grew up in the shadow of the Cascades, and I spent many of my childhood camping trips and vacations, perhaps even parts of all of them, visiting different mountainous regions. Today my wife and I make our home in a small town close to Mt. Rainier, and when I look out my back window, I can see the 14,411- foot giant volcano rising majestically above the local landscape.

When my job transferred me to Salt Lake City, I used to spend as many summer mornings as possible up at the top of Big Cottonwood Canyon in the Wasatch mountain range. There at the top of the canyon (approximately nine thousand feet), I would walk to the far side of Silver Lake and watch as the early morning sun rose over the peaks and sparkled on the still surface of the water. It was quiet, peaceful, and it felt like the top of the world. It was a great way to start the day before heading to work. For me, being up high in the peaks really does feel otherworldly, which matches some of ancient humanity's mythical view of mountains.

One particularly memorable mountain experience in my life comes from the time Chris and I spent in Switzerland. It was the middle of June, and snow still covered many of the mountaintops, providing us with some gorgeous vistas. From the views, the atmosphere, and the mood, I'd have to say that our experience of the Alps was phenomenal. I've been to higher mountain ranges—many peaks in the Rockies, Uintas, Wasatch, and Cascades top out at higher elevations than many peaks in the Alps—but the magnitude and abruptness of the Alps is both unique and stunning. Their rapid rise to dramatic heights really imparts a sense of grandeur, and the other ranges I've visited, while fabulous in their own ways, just don't match them.

Driving south out of Germany, we decided to spend our first night in Switzerland at Braunwald, a tiny Swiss village perched high on a mountainside with no road access. Not wanting to hike all the way up the mountain with our luggage, we took advantage of the local funicular (a cable railway that ascends steep inclines). Upon our arrival, a horse-drawn cart carried us even farther up the mountainside, passing through vivid green meadows punctuated with bright clusters of tiny mountain flowers. As the daylight slowly turned to dusk, we sat outside on the hotel balcony enjoying authentic Swiss fondue while gazing at the rising mountain pass in front of us. In planning our trip for the next day, we decided we would drive up and over the winding Klausenpass road in order to see the deep, high reaches of the mountain pass.

After a contemplative stroll through the meadows the next morning, we descended back down and began the long, nervous drive up the narrow, twisting roads. When we finally approached the top of the pass, it felt as if we were visiting the very top of the world. We parked the car along the shoulder and decided to explore a bit. Looking out across this last high point, we saw that we were in a long, narrow valley that ran alongside a tall, formidable cliff. The mountains continued to rise above the top of the cliffs, which then disappeared into the clouds. The valley floor was a beautiful color of green dissected by several tiny, white streams of glacial runoff. It looked like a slice of paradise (for a mountain-lover like me), and it provoked a feeling of otherworldliness. It didn't feel like a natural place for humans to be—it was too high, too drastic, and too separated from the rest of humanity and from normal human experience. It was a marvelous, magical place. At the far end of the valley, the very last rise in the road stood just a few hundred feet above the rest of the valley. Eventually we got back in the car and continued to drive the length of the valley floor while taking in as much of the scenery as possible. As we approached the crest of that final hill and were just a few car lengths from the very top of the pass, we came to a sudden stop: several large boulders had just come loose from the mountainside above and rolled across the road a few cars in front of us. They would have crushed any vehicle in their path like a Swiss cow stepping on a mountain flower. It was a bit unsettling, and it really did have the feel of a divine warning: it was an action that ancient people would have perceived as the mountain spirits warning mere humans to stay away from this area so close to the upper realm of the divine. The ancients believed the mountains were potential abodes for the divine, and humans only entered by the permission of the divine or at their own extreme risk.

Mountainous Axis Mundi

With their highest peaks sparkling in the sun or blanketed by a high layer of clouds, the visual image of the mountain seems to naturally express itself as a point of connection between heaven and earth, which is exactly why the ancients often viewed them as an axis mundi.[119] They also share a similar feature with stone: they appear to be relatively absolute and immutable, which is a key aspect of many hierophanies and axis mundi. In addition to that, their high elevation puts the tops of their peaks "closer to God," or at least closer to the upper realm of the divine. It is no surprise that ancient people sometimes viewed the mountains as part of a sky epiphany. One special aspect of a mountain as a point of connection is that the holy peak itself may occasionally be an accessible axis mundi (to some extent). If the gods either live at the top of the mountain, or if they visit there from time to time, then the slopes of the mountain form the "ladder" by which one can climb to the top (ascend closer to the heavens) and commune with the sacred. That's not to say that every single mountaintop was necessarily a place of divine manifestation. There were many profane mountain peaks and hilltops, and to the best of our knowledge, only a few of which were holy. However, each peak represented an opportunity for divine manifestation, and wherever the divine manifested in the form of a mountaintop hierophany, the mountain then became a point of sacred connection.

As with standing stones, the concept of the mountain as a place of possible connection to the divine was very widespread among ancient cultures. We need only think back to the famous Greek epics to remember the peak of Mt. Olympus as a place where the gods lived, and it was a point of connection between the heavens and the earth. This legendary home of the gods wasn't just any ordinary mountain peak. According to *The Iliad*, it was on the *highest* peak.[120] A similar pattern also presented itself elsewhere in the cultures of that region. The Greek *omphalos* was a hill (or sometimes a mountain-shaped stone) that signified a sacred center and point of connection with the Divine.[121] In fact, one of the earliest known sites of worship for Zeus, the sky deity, is found at an altar on Mount Lykaion.[122]

This mountaintop pattern was not limited to the area of the Aegean Sea. For many of the people in Asia, Mount Meru served as an axis mundi and a point of sacred connection. Over time and cultural evolution, it continued to be valued as such in parts of the mythologies of Hindus, Buddhists, and Jains.[123] Sung-shan was a sacred mountain in China, one of five specific cosmic mountains in the Taoist traditions.[124] Elsewhere, the Norse had Himingbjör, which was a world mountain[125] and contained all of the symbolism and religious importance of the other mountains that served as axis mundi.[126] Examples of this pattern of thought continued through the Americas, Africa, and the rest of Asia, but we won't belabor the point by listing them all here.

This is also true for the cultures of the ancient Middle East (and therefore for the immediate cultural context of the ancient authors of scripture). The Epic of Gilgamesh refers to Enlil, the father of the gods, as being associated with a mountain.[127] Hara Berezaiti is the cosmic mountain mentioned in the Avesta (ancient Zoroastrian scriptures).[128] Michael Heiser's excellent book, *The Unseen Realm*, references Ugaritic beliefs about mountains that also cross over into the Bible, such as Og, the King of Bashan, ruling from a place of spiritual authority in the area containing Mount Hermon. Mt. Hermon has a history of supernatural activity and in modern times is a site of significant conflict between Syria and Israel.[129] An Ugaritic poem unearthed in Ras Shamra talks about Baal being taken to the "*heights* of the North."[130] Continuing in the modern Middle East, Islam teaches that Muhammed ascended up into heaven from the top of the Temple Mount in Jerusalem,[131] a place which was clearly renowned as a spiritual center. Devout Muslims built one of their holiest sites on this location: the famous Dome of the Rock. The ancient patterns still hold true today. In the past few years, a conflict over Mauna Kea in Hawaii has come up between scientists and native Hawaiians. Scientists want to place a fancy telescope on the top of the mountain; however, the mountain is a place of worship "where the sky and earth meet," and it is a place the gods created in order to ascend up into the heavens.[132]

Manufactured Mountains

We should also note that people created human imitations of mountains in the form of pyramid-like temples. Tall, stone temples stretching up above the population center served as a place where a person could commune with the sacred (sacred connection). After all, that's the essential the purpose of a temple: it provides a connection to the upper realm so humankind can communicate with the divine.[133] It was not a coincidence that people all over the world created mountain-shaped temples. The temple of Borobudur mentioned in the introductory chapter of this book was a human imitation of Mount Meru,[134] and a person's ascent up the temple was equivalent to journeying to a sacred center.[135] The Babylonians referred to their temples as "Mountain of the House of God," "Link between heaven and earth," and in other similar fashions. Their ziggurat (pyramid temple) was a mountainous axis mundi, which, by way of ascent, enabled the priest to enter a point of connection with the upper realm.[136] The Mesopotamians endorsed this concept of the temple as a point of sacred connection. They often assumed their temples were a home for the gods much in the same way that we have a physical building as a place of residence as humans.[137] The Sumerian word *ḫarsag* refers to a mountain house that is a temple. It has an explicit link that runs from the underworld, through the human realm, and up into the heavens.[138]

Holy Mountains in Scripture

The pattern of a mountain as a place of sacred connection, and the construction of pyramid-shaped temples as human imitations, was a very common ancient pattern, including in the cultures that surrounded the early people of scripture. Worshipping pagan deities in these "high places" was a common practice in that part of the world, and this form of idolatry plagued the Israelites as they veered back and forth between the unholy and the righteous. The prophet Jeremiah lamented the widespread worship of false gods when he described the pagan practices of the Israelites. "On *every high hill* and under every green tree you have lain down as a harlot" (Jeremiah 2:20, emphasis added). Hosea wrote of idolatrous worship at high places when he wrote, "They offer sacrifices *on the tops of the mountains* and burn incense *on the hills*" (Hosea 4:13, emphasis added). 2 Chronicles 14:3 refers to these "foreign altars and *high places*," as do many other passages (emphasis added).

However, not all of the examples we find in the Bible are negative. A psalm attributed to the sons of Korah describes "... *His holy mountain. Beautiful in elevation, the joy of the whole earth, is Mount Zion* on the sides of the north, the city of the great King. God is in her palaces, He is known as her refuge" (Psalm 48:1b-3, emphasis added). This song clearly depicts Mount Zion as a cosmic mountain. Note the passage describes it as "beautiful in elevation," how it is relevant for "the whole earth," and how the Divine dwells there. Psalm 99:9 contains an instruction to "Exalt the LORD our God and worship at His holy hill" (a passage well-known from a climactic moment in *The Englishman Who Went Up A Hill But Came Down A Mountain*, a film that communicates the subconscious value people place on mountains).

We can see other examples of this style of thought by looking at the life of Moses. When Moses was tending the flock of his father-in-law, Jethro, he "came to Horeb, *the mountain of God*" (Exodus 3:1, emphasis added). Later, during the Exodus from Egypt, God Himself told Moses to "be ready in the morning, and *come up* in the morning to *Mount Sinai*, and present yourself to Me there on the *top of the mountain*" (Exodus 34:2, emphasis added). Both of these stories describe mountains in the cosmic tradition and as axis mundi.

During the construction of the first temple, tradition relates that Solomon actually raised the area of land they were building on (the Temple Mount) so that it would be level with the top of a nearby mountain. This would have been no easy task, but then, in the traditional mode of ancient thought, the sacred temple of God had to be at least as high in elevation as the other locations in the immediate vicinity. Josephus described this when he wrote that the builders "had elevated the ground four hundred cubits, he made it to be on a level with the top of the mountain, on which the temple was built."[139]

In the New Testament, Matthew wrote that right before the Transfiguration, Jesus "led them up on a high mountain" (Matthew 17:1b). On what we now call "the Mount of Transfiguration," Jesus' face shined and he appeared as if he was clothed with robes like white light. Moses and Elijah—long since gone—appeared with him, and God spoke audibly from the heavens (Matthew 17:1-9). In another example found at the end of the Bible, John's vision of the end times depicts Mount Zion as a place of the Divine and as a place of special sanctuary for those loyal to and set apart for God. "Then I looked, and behold, the Lamb was standing on Mount Zion, and with Him one hundred and forty-four thousand, having His name and the name of His Father written on their foreheads" (Revelation 14:1).

These are just a few examples taken from the many passages of scripture that confirm the biblical validity of the concept of a mountainous axis mundi. While people violated and perverted this in pursuit of pagan practices, God, whatever His reasons might be, personally established the pattern of the mountainous axis mundi. It wasn't the only pattern He would establish.

☙ CHAPTER 10: ❧

Trees

AS A YOUNG BOY, I was no different from the other kids at school in that I loved to climb trees. There was something special about ascending up in the air and seeing the world from a different perspective. I couldn't do it at home though, since the trees in my backyard were either too big and had no low branches for climbing or they were too small and the branches were too fragile to support a child (although I tried). However, my friend who lived a few blocks away had a couple of great climbing trees in his front yard, and we climbed them often. In one tall tree, there was a small treehouse with just enough room to sit. The other tree was shorter, but the branches were perfect for climbing, and it was easy to climb through the whole tree without fear of falling. As young kids, we invented a number of games to play in the trees. The only downside was the pitch all over your hands and clothes when you were done.

Whether fifteen or fifty feet off the ground, when I climbed high among the branches of a tree, it felt as if I had entered another realm entirely. There is something special about trees, and it's exciting to sit high among the living branches surrounded by needles or leaves. Many years later, when I was adult, I happened to be driving down the road where my friend's house was. I had not been there in decades, and I looked over to glance at the familiar home as I drove by. I had to stop the car and look hard for the house. It should have been the second one in from the corner, but something was off about it, and I didn't recognize the house immediately. Then I saw it: the house was there, but the trees were gone, and now the front yard was empty. It may seem silly, but I felt a twinge of sorrow at the passing of those trees. I loved climbing them.

We see the same feeling of enthusiasm in a television show my family enjoys watching. *Treehouse Masters* follows Pete Nelson and his team of carpenters extraordinaire as they travel around the country building fantastic tree houses for various clients. Working high in the trees, they have constructed a recording studio, a bar, a writing refuge, and several other special dwellings high up in the canopy. Watching the show, you can tell that Pete feels a special connection with the trees, and his clients almost universally gain a new appreciation for the trees and for experiencing familiar terrain from a fresh, elevated perspective among the boughs of a living organism. Technically none of those tree houses are very high off of the ground, but it's still enough of an elevation change to make it feel like you are closer to the realm of the sky.

Sacrality, Life, and Renewal

Much like scaling the side of a sacred mountain or ascending a temple, climbing a tree is also an ascent that can symbolically represent entry into the upper realm. After all, the branches of a tree are far above the ground, and they belong more to the realm of the birds than to humans (and birds are often part of sky epiphanies). As a result, sacred trees as points of hierophanic connection have occupied a special place in spiritual thought through the ages. Like their megalithic counterparts, sacred trees bury their roots in and under the earth (symbolizing a connection to the underworld). They pass through the earthly realm of humankind, and then they stretch upward toward the heavens.[140] People often lived in relative proximity to trees, which made them easily and universally accessible as a symbol. Juniper, balsam, or redwood, the type of tree didn't matter so much to ancient people as simply having a sacred tree.

Just as the megalithic representations of sacred connection make use of the qualities of stone, the existential aspect of a tree brings a special quality to any axis mundi it represents. We might recall that stone, with its hard and unchanging nature, represents the absolute nature of the divine manifestation. Does a tree communicate the same thing? The answer is "partially." As is true of all hierophanies, the tree-related hierophany communicates absolute truth and existence by its hierophanic nature, but the use of a tree to represent the point of sacred connection does not call to mind the hard, unchanging aspect of stone. Rather, the symbolic aspect of a tree represents the source and renewal of life.[141] Stones are relatively unchanging, but many trees undergo regular change. All trees reflect growth and life, and deciduous trees are especially great examples. These trees are barren in the winter, grow tiny, green buds in the spring, the buds turn to full, green leaves in the summer, which then turn to other brilliant colors in the fall, and then they die and fall to the ground, after which the renewal of life can begin via seeds, decomposition, and nutrient replenishment. Obviously, the nature of a tree does not naturally communicate the absolute, immutable nature of the divine as stone does. While the tree is a living, changing axis mundi, it still contains all of the same underlying, implicit truths as any other hierophanic center with regard to connection and central importance. But, rather than emphasizing the absolute, sacred trees often emphasized aspects related to life, birth, regeneration, and fertility (similar to mother-goddess imagery in pagan belief systems).[142] A hierophantic center possessing the existential qualities of both stones and trees should be familiar attributes for Christians: the divine as the origin of absolute, unchanging truth as well as the source and renewal of life.

Sacred Trees from around the World

The combination of the tree and axis mundi seemed to imprint itself naturally on human thinking as symbols of sacred trees (often referred to as "cosmic" or "world" trees) were found all over the world.[143] This includes examples both ancient and relatively recent. One instance of the use of sacred trees comes from the ancient cultures of the area of modern India.[144] From the fifteenth chapter of the *Bhagavad Gita*, Krishna, "the Blessed Lord," speaks of the "world tree," which is an archetypical cosmic tree/axis mundi.[145] The *Bhagavad Gita* itself is a written record of a critical Hindu hierophany as this portion of their scriptures tells of the manifestation of the Ultimate Reality/Brahman (God/Krishna) and his appearance to the Hindu devotee Arjuna. Also arising out of Indian philosophical and religious traditions, Buddhist history teaches that Siddhartha Guatama (the Buddha) achieved his famous enlightenment while sitting under a tree, and as a result, this tree acquired a high level of sacred significance.[146] That he was sitting under a tree was probably not a coincidence; it was likely an adaptation of the pattern of a hierophany applied to a tree. Outside of that region, both Arctic and Pacific native cultures, though separated by many miles, have a cosmic tree whose branches reach into the heavens.[147] Sacred trees are prevalent throughout Iroquois myth as well.[148] Found in an ancient Germanic tradition in the *Hávamál*, a portion of the Poetic Edda, the god Odin sacrificed himself on a tree. It is clearly a world tree as it "rises to heaven."[149] Not to be left out, Chinese mythology also makes use of a sacred tree, as do many other cultures.[150]

Sacred trees were also particularly important to an entire mode of magico-religious expression and ritual. A critical part of shamanistic religion is the shaman's ability to ascend into the upper realm (symbolically), and sometimes they accomplished this sacred ascent by climbing a ritually consecrated tree. Even in the mid-1800s, the shamans of the Altaic Turks continued to use this method. In their spiritual practices, the shaman symbolically climbed a sacred tree to enter into the presence of their supreme deity, Bai Ulgan.[151]

This form of sacred connection as represented by special trees also held true in the cultures that were part of the biblical landscape. Assyria had a cosmic tree, as noted by monuments associated with the biblical town of Nineveh.[152] This tree was also found on The Seal of *Sin-aḫ-uṣur*, a neo-Assyrian seal. It shows the god Assur being supported by a sacred tree.[153] The Babylonians also had a sacred tree.[154] Egyptian mythology even had a "Tree of Life" (that might sound familiar to Christians).[155] Sacred trees held great spiritual value for people all over the world, and their role of sacred connection in ancient thought is widespread—even in the cultures that surrounded the ancient authors of scripture.

Trees as Biblical Symbols

The people of Israel seemed to embrace the concept of sacred trees when they turned aside from God and worshipped pagan gods. For example, during the reign of some evil kings, they set up pagan items "under every green tree" (2 Kings 17:10b). The prophet Jeremiah uses a similar phrase, but he adds some extra emphasis to his condemnation. "Under every green tree you have lain down as a harlot" (Jeremiah 2:20b). The harlot remark indicates that the Israelites had committed spiritual adultery by worshipping false gods, and notes they performed their pagan practices or built their shrines under trees. These are two examples of false sacred trees in the Bible, but there is at least one example of a sacred tree in the Bible that is not false.

You may have already thought of a biblical example of a sacred tree since most people are probably familiar with the story of the Garden of Eden, and the Tree of Life takes a position of central importance in that story. We're going to look at the story of the Garden of Eden in much more detail later on, but we'll take a quick look at the Tree of Life right now. The Tree of Life is an archetypical cosmic tree, and in many ways, it is *the* definitive axis mundi and center. It was supernatural by nature, and it reflected the aspects of life giving and renewal. When Adam could eat from the tree, he lived. When Adam could not eat from the tree, he became subject to death. This is a perfect symbol of humanity's relationship with God. When people lived in perfect communion and connection with God (who is the source of all life), we lived. After we lost that connection with God via sin, we died (literally and spiritually).

The last chapter of the Bible (Revelation 22) mentions the Tree of Life several more times, and this comes at the point when the full connection with God is re-established and life (eternal) is once again available to redeemed humankind. In this way, the Tree of Life maintains all of the general underlying patterns of a sacred center and axis mundi, but it also adds the aspects that are partly specific to the pattern of a sacred tree. The axis mundi (which represents the divine) is more than just an absolute orientation for living. The divine, which it represents, is both the ultimate *cause* and *continuation* of life itself. To remain in communion with the divine is to live; to fall out of communion with the divine is to die. This is perfectly consistent with the life-giving and life-sustaining aspects of the archetypical cosmic tree. This also sets the stage for the second biblical form of the tree (or rather it is a *symbol* of a cosmic tree): The Cross. We won't go into detail on the topic of the Cross quite yet, but we'll look at it very closely as we progress further.

CHAPTER 11:

Staff and Pole

I GREW UP WITH A love for great stories of fiction. When I was in the second grade, I remember checking out a copy of J.R.R. Tolkien's masterful book of child's fantasy, *The Hobbit*, from the library at Maplewood Elementary School in Puyallup. I read it quickly, and it fascinated something in my childhood mind. As soon as I finished it, I wanted to read *The Lord of the Rings*, Tolkien's large follow-up tale to *The Hobbit*. Our school library had two sections: one that had books for the younger group, first through third grade, and then another section for those in the fourth grade and above. *The Lord of the Rings* is a more difficult read than *The Hobbit*, and the library workers placed it in the section for older students. When I went to check out the trilogy of books, the librarian prevented me on the basis that it was too difficult to read at my age. Disheartened, I went home without the books. Soon afterward, I looked around at my dad's bookshelf, and he had a copy of the trilogy sitting on the top shelf. With the aid of a chair to stand on, I pulled them down, being particularly determined to conquer these books since I was recently denied access to them.

What a fantastic, wonderful world these books revealed! Archetypical, mythical constructs of good and evil battled for the very fate of the world. The spiritual, mythical elements are clear for anyone with an eye to see them. While Tolkien explicitly denies having put any deliberate, specific symbolism in the books, he did explain that he wanted to create a mythology for Britain. As a professor and linguistic scholar, he spent many years translating and teaching about some of ancient Europe's epic myths, and he wanted to give something similar back to Britain. As such, it is no wonder that many mythical, symbolic patterns, if not specific particulars, manifested in his writing. Though fantasy, two memorable moments from *The Lord of the Rings* introduce us to the role of the staff as a symbol of connection with the Divine. In the story, the five wizards (who were essentially angelic emissaries sent from the gods) each had a staff, and these staffs seemed to be a connection to their divinely given powers. When Gandalf faced the demonic Balrog on the bridge in Moria, he broke the bridge using divine powers by striking it with his staff.[156] Later in the story, the fallen wizard Saruman spoke of the staffs of wizards in terms that equated them to the crowns of kings—symbols of their power and authority.[157] When Gandalf exercised his divinely given authority[158] and cast the fallen Saruman out of the order of wizards, thus stripping him of his power and divine connection, he pointedly told Saruman that he was removing him from the order and that he was breaking his staff, which then of course immediately broke into pieces and became useless.[159] The wizards were not deities themselves; they were that fictional world's closest equivalent to angels. As such they did not possess intrinsic power. Their powers came from somewhere else (God/ Eru Ilúvatar), and it could be taken away from them, as it was with Saruman. The staff was their symbol of divine connection, a conduit of sorts, and they drew upon that connection to the Divine.

Portable Axis Mundi

Back in our real world, part of a shaman's initiation involves an ascent to heaven.[160] Many shamanic practices involved the shaman's ascent to heaven on an axis mundi, which sometimes made use of an actual sacred tree placed inside of a holy building. However, they often used a pole to replace the tree in these sacred rituals. A pole, trunk, or branch was obviously much easier to handle than an entire tree, especially when the holy rituals needed to take place inside of a building (often a tent, yurt, or some equivalent). Like other symbolic representations of a center, a pole is a vertical object that one plants in the ground (hence, it reaches to the underworld). It passes through the human realm and ends above the human up in the sky. The pole found in so many dwelling places was more than just efficient engineering. The move toward ease of use and portability indicated the ongoing human desire to live close and in relation to the divine wherever the people currently lived. We can see this central role of the sacred pole or pillar in dwellings all over the world. The Baiga claimed that their shaman's ascent into the sky involved a pole.[161] Far to the north and across the vast expanse of the Atlantic, the center pole found in the homes of North American and Arctic natives specifically represented a sacred center.[162]

Ease of transport and use was particularly important for people who were constantly moving to new locations. For the nomadic people in ancient Siberia and central Asia, the pole often replaced the tree in shamanic rituals. Use of either tree or pole was acceptable.[163] However, most poles were of a wooden variety and people often took them from a holy tree. If a nomadic people witnessed a hierophany centered on a tree, then the best way to preserve their contact with the sacred was to take a symbolic axis mundi (pole) directly from the original, hierophanically consecrated axis mundi (tree). This allowed them to carry their sacred point of connection with them at all times.

The portable pole could also be a handheld staff. For example, the Achilpa employed this form of sacred connection quite explicitly. They believed that their supreme deity, Numbakula, specifically made a sacred pole from the trunk of a tree that he had used to climb into the upper realm (note the tree as the connection point between realms). The humans Numbakula created carried that pole with them, and it allowed them to maintain their connection with the divine regardless of their physical location in the world.[164] In one story, the Achilpa lost their staff, meaning they no longer had a way to connect with the Divine. Knowing what the lost connection truly meant for them, they simply laid down to die.[165] That is a serious form of devotion to the divine connection!

Far away from Australia in pre-Hispanic Mesoamerica, we still see similar examples of this thought demonstrated by the shamans who lived there.[166] A ruler's scepter is another expression of divine connection and authority, and the scepter became a common symbol of the divine right of kings and queens stretching from the ancient Middle East to recent royal history in Europe. Even in modern fiction like *The Lord of the Rings*, the staff often represents a mystical connection with the divine. A magician's wand is probably similar.

In the cultures that surrounded the authors of the Bible, a common form of pagan worship condemned in the scriptures involved Asherah poles. In continuing the patterns discussed, the poles may have been an alternative for trees. Sometimes they were full-sized pillars carved out of wood.[167] Asherah may also have been the name of a deity worshipped by his followers who used poles as part of their rituals.[168] This was a danger for the people of Israel. The instructions in Deuteronomy 16:21 specifically forbid the use of an Asherah next to an altar of the Lord. King Ahab used this pagan method as he "also made the Asherah. Ahab did more to provoke the LORD God of Israel than all the kings of Israel who were before him" (1 Kings 16:33). Manasseh did the same, invoking God's wrath in the process (2 Kings 21:3-16). Josiah later tore down all the Asherah poles in accordance with God's law (2 Kings 23), which was righteous. People used these poles in all sorts of pagan worship, and often as part of fertility rituals.[169] The maypole is a probable example of this as it was probably originally a pagan practice celebrating and inviting fertility and a fruitful planting and growth season. It lost its original pagan meaning over time and became commonplace throughout Europe, even in modern times. The wooden pole or staff continued some of the same sense of life giving and renewal that was also part of the symbol of sacred trees.

The Staff in the Bible

We have already seen several examples of sacred poles or staffs as representing sacred connection and (portable) centers from various religions throughout history. However, these practices were not unique to the rituals and beliefs of those who served false gods. In fact, some of the great stories of scripture provide the best examples of this pattern of sacred behavior. We'll return to the story of Moses for these examples.

When God told Moses to go to Pharaoh and secure the release of his people, Moses asked God, "What if they will not believe me or listen to what I say? For they may say, 'The LORD has not appeared to you'" (Exodus 4:1). God heard Moses voice a concern that people may not believe that he had actually been in the presence of God and was directly commissioned by Him. Moses feared that people would choose to believe that he did not have any real divine authority. In response, God used the staff of Moses as the sign of his divinely ordained authority. In doing this, God made use of a clear, ancient symbol that showed Moses had connection with the Divine. God instructed Moses, "You shall take in your hand this staff, with which you shall perform the signs" (Exodus 4:17). The signs were not things that Moses could do himself; the signs were of a supernatural nature; they did not originate with humans. By using the staff to perform the signs, it indicated that the source of the signs was God, and that Moses served Him in this mission. This divine connection and authority, as indicated by the holy staff, became quite clear when God's prophets, Moses and Aaron, faced off against Pharaoh and his spiritual advisors.

> Now the LORD spoke to Moses and Aaron, saying, "When Pharaoh speaks to you, saying 'Work a miracle,' then you shall say to Aaron, 'Take your staff and throw it down before Pharaoh, that it may become a serpent.'" So Moses and Aaron came to Pharaoh, and thus they did just as the LORD had commanded; and Aaron threw his staff down before Pharaoh and his servants, and it became a serpent. Then Pharaoh also called for the wise men and the sorcerers, and they also, the magicians of Egypt, did the same with their secret arts. For each one threw down his staff and they turned into serpents. But Aaron's staff swallowed up their staffs (Exodus 7:8-12).

In this story both the prophet's and magician's staffs indicated connection with supernatural powers. However, the God of Israel demonstrated His superiority when Aaron's staff eliminated the Egyptian magician's staffs. The sacred connection of Moses and Aaron pointed to the absolute, divine authority of God, while the magicians of Pharaoh lost their symbol of connection to their pagan deities. This demonstrated that absolute truth and true sacred connection lie with God, which the portable axis mundi of Moses and Aaron pointed toward. Note there was no divinity in the staff itself, and neither Moses nor Aaron possessed that quality either. The staff simply pointed to the divine source just like any other axis mundi. The staff served as a center point of connection and reference.

After Moses led the Israelites out of Egypt, they found themselves trapped between Pharaoh's army and the Red Sea with no way to escape the coming slaughter. God delivered them from this destruction by a display of absolute, divine power: He parted the Red Sea.[170] This allowed the Israelites to cross safely to the other side, and then the sea rushed back in and drowned the Egyptian armies. In parting the Red Sea, God instructed Moses to "*lift up your staff* and stretch out your hand over the sea" (Exodus 14:16a, emphasis added). Once again, in this story of divine power and deliverance, the staff is an axis mundi; it is a symbolic connection to the Divine. God performed the miraculous work, not Moses, but Moses held the symbol of connection and authority, which he raised up toward the sky.

After crossing the Red Sea and while they were wandering in the desert, the refugees ended up in dire need of water. Once more, the power of the divine (and the authority of Moses to lead the people as God's chosen representative) was on display via the use of a staff. "Take in your hand your staff with which you struck the Nile, and go. Behold, I will stand before you there on the rock at Horeb; and you shall strike the rock, and water will come out of it" (Exodus 17:5b-6a). Note that God says, "I will stand before you there on the rock." That's clearly an example of a hierophany and of sacred connection. And once again the life-giving and sustaining power of the divine is on display as water rushes forth to nourish the people.

We can see another example during the battle between the Amalekites and the refugees. In preparation for this battle, Moses told Joshua to go ahead and fight the enemies, and Moses said he was going to "station myself on the *top of the hill* with *the staff of God* in my hand" (Exodus 17:9b, emphasis added). The Bible relates that it was a very long battle, and that Israel won the battle when Moses held his up his hand, *with the staff of God in it,* toward the upper realm. However, Israel began to lose when Moses grew tired and was unable to hold it up. When the staff, which was a symbol of the connection with the divine, was raised toward the heavens (in obvious appeal to God), God supported the people in the battle. When the staff was lowered (away from the divine and down toward the merely profane), the divine aid was lost.

In each of the last three examples in which God saved his people (the division of the Red Sea, water from the rock, and victory over the Amalekites), God commanded Moses to use the portable axis mundi as an integral part of the human ritual. This axis mundi represented God as the source and continuation of their life, and therefore it was a symbolic center. The symbols and rituals themselves had no intrinsic value—hitting a rock with a piece of wood is generally meaningless—but the use of the symbols is part of how God taught key concepts to the ancient Israelites. These are the same concepts we're learning as we examine these stories.

We'll look at one final example before we move on. It also takes place during the Exodus at a point when deadly serpents were biting the Israelites. In response to the calamity, God told Moses to put a bronze serpent on a pole and raise it up before the people. People suffering from a venomous bite who wanted to live simply had to raise their eyes to look at the serpent on top of the pole. If they did this, God healed them (Numbers 21:4-9). In this final example, God used the pole (as an axis mundi) to indicate that life and renewal come from Him. The approved, biblical use of the concept of an axis mundi (valid when it points to God) is again clear.

Summarizing the Symbols of the Center

It's fun to look at the wide variety of religious expressions found all over the ancient world and find that the people of scripture used the same patterns to represent sacred connection. Concepts of sacrality and connection as expressed through the use of stones, mountains, trees, and staffs are common in the Bible, although many modern people don't recognize them as such. The widespread application of the ancient patterns is evidence that people universally valued the concept of centers (composed of axis mundi, hierophanies, and sacred connection) even if the particulars of each religious system were different from one another.

In all cases, the symbolic representation of the axis mundi marked a potential connection between realms. The implied hierophany provided guidance and a reference point for living. But, significant symbolism did not end with stones, mountains, and trees. The ancient people also employed forms of symbolism that pointed to the most impactful display of divine power, and yet this form of symbolism may be the most difficult for modern people to recognize, even though it's all around us. Let's explore this next.

ᄿᯤ CHAPTER 12: ᯤᯤ

Creation and Cosmogony

WE HAVE A FAMILY OFFICE in our home where Chris, Ephraim, and I keep computers, printers, scanners, and other similar equipment. We each have a desktop workstation set up in the office, and in the far corner we mounted a television so we can work on our computers and also watch whatever happens to be on TV. It's an active, busy room that is usually quite noisy, with the sounds of videos, games, music, and TV coming from several sources at the same time. But late in the evening of March 10, 2011, around 10:45 p.m. (PST), our office became noticeably quieter.

Ephraim was asleep in bed, and Chris and I were in the office working on our computers while we had one of the national news channels playing on the TV. The news broke into their regular programming with a developing story: a massive earthquake had hit Japan, and water was rising rapidly along the coast. We watched the live and near-live feeds as massive surges of water poured over sea walls, rushed across roads, and tore through houses. It was horrifying. As we witnessed the long, live, unedited video feed from the NHK news helicopter flying over the Miyagi Prefecture, the only sounds we made were groans of despair as we watched the waves racing toward people who were trying unsuccessfully to flee. From the vantage point of the helicopter high up in the air, we could see that most of the people trying to escape the oncoming wave would not survive, and there was nothing anyone could do about it. The power of the sea to cause destruction, its utter inescapability, and the complete helplessness of its victims, was a horrible reality made explicitly clear over those moments. It was truly awful.

As we processed what we were seeing, Chris, who had read some of my earlier research on sea symbolism, mentioned that she now really understood how the ancient people could have viewed the sea as a chaotic, destructive evil that was too powerful for humans to overcome. We had just witnessed it.

A couple of years later, I was on a "bro-trip" with Brent, my brother-in-law (Chris's brother). At that time, we both worked for the same large company (though in different divisions), and by sheer coincidence we were both at different stages of our respective business trips. I had just spent a week in the UK and was returning home, and he was flying out to spend a couple of weeks in India. Both of our flights routed through the Frankfurt airport within an hour of each other, and so we decided to spend some of our accumulated vacation time and personal money to take advantage of the fortuitous schedule. On our own dime, we extended our Frankfurt layover by a week or so, rented a car, and commenced a road trip through parts of continental Europe.

At one point, we ended up in my favorite city, Salzburg. In my previous trips to Europe, I spent time visiting lots of cathedrals, so I no longer went into every cathedral that I saw unless I knew there was something particularly special about it. On this particular day, Brent really wanted to visit Der Salzburger Dom (The Salzburg Cathedral), and for some reason I had never gone inside of it before. I acquiesced to his request, and soon we went inside. As our eyes adjusted to the light and we looked around, I saw a baptismal font in the back corner to our left. I have a special fondness for the baptism ritual, so I went over to check it out. Soon my casual interest turned into full-blown obsession.

The baptismal font sat on a stone platform consisting of two perpendicular, crossing stone arms, as if it was resting on the lines representing the four directions of the compass. Sitting on top of each stone arm was a lion made from metal. The large, cast-metal baptismal font rested on the back of these four lions. With the first glance, I immediately recognized the deep symbolism used in the construction of this structure as it relates to water rituals, but as I drew closer it got even better. The lid of this cast-metal structure (perhaps bronze?) displayed several basic, etched-line pictures. These pictures covered the lid and told a progressive story as I walked around the baptismal font in a circle. It told its tale using pictures of water stories and related symbolism found in the Bible, from Creation, to Noah, to the Egyptians swallowed by the sea, to Jesus speaking to the woman at the well. I immediately went into full-on religious-geek mode, talking incessantly to Brent as I tried to quickly explain the history of water symbolism in religion, starting with the idea of the chaotic, evil, dangerous sea (as exemplified by recent events like the tsunami in Japan) and culminating in displays of God's power. He listened dutifully and politely over the next several days as I kept returning to the topic with the passion of a true religion and theology nerd. After all, he was trapped in the rental car with me and could not flee the verbal onslaught of obscure religious facts.

A few days later, we chanced across the Celtic and Roman ruins of Glanum, which is south of Saint-Rémy in Provence. By chance, Glanum had a local Celtic water cult as the basis for its origin and prosperity.[171] As we visited the ancient spring and sacred buildings erected near the site, we discussed the presence of water rituals again. I think seeing this presence and prevalence across multiple locations and cultures combined to serve as a reminder of how powerful and pervasive water symbolism was for the people of the older world.

The Power of the Divine on Full Display

All ancient societies had stories that explained the origin of the world and the arrival of human life. In academic terms, these are known as cosmogonic myths. We're going to use variations on the word *cosmogony* fairly often as we proceed through the rest of this book, so let's define it here: cosmogony is the theory of the cause of the existence of the world, which often included the origin of human life. If you remember the word as being roughly equal to creation or dealing with creation mythologies, then you'll do okay.

These creation stories served a particular purpose: to tell people what happened, why things happened, and explain how the world ended up the way it is. It often justified a particular society's social structure and rules.[172] For example, Christians looked to the first few chapters of Genesis and the story of the Garden of Eden not only for an explanation of the fact of existence, but also to understand the human experience of existence, which is a life of separation from God (the Fall of humanity).

Most early myths taught that the world was not quite ready for human habitation immediately after creation.[173] The divine needed to take some additional action in order to make it ready for humans. Sometimes this action or series of actions was taken quite soon after creation, but in other stories it didn't take place until after some amount of time had passed. Either way, it required a tremendous amount of *raw supernatural power* to do these things (creation and life). The early people held this manifestation of power to be of great importance. As a result, cosmogonic thought is found throughout ancient cultures, including in the Bible. In fact, there is quite a multitude of cosmogonic symbols in scripture, but many of them are subtle enough that most people aren't aware of how pervasive they are. While it's out of scope for this work, cataloging the multitude of these symbols would be a fascinating study, and it would be larger and more detailed than most people would realize. Water plays an important role in many of these stories or symbols.

Regarding the human view of water, we all know it is something we need for our survival, and some ancient thought regarding water, particularly freshwater streams, rivers, and lakes, reflects its critical role in human survival. There is no denying that some religious thought about water reflected the positive impact it had on people's lives. For example, Jesus once spoke to a woman drawing water from a local well and told her that he provided a different water that had an eternal benefit (John 4:14).

But aside from that, some bodies of water like the oceans and seas were intimidating and confusing for ancient people. They didn't always understand why oceans could be so dangerous and unpredictable. Modern science helps us understand things about the seas that ancient people didn't necessarily know back then. We know that our planet is round, that the universe does not center on the third planet from the Sun, and that complex interactions of gravity, heat, winds, geography, and other natural, humanly understandable factors drive the movement of the earth's seas. Even then, there is much we cannot anticipate (tsunamis), and when we are able to predict something like the arrival of a terrible storm (Hurricane Katrina), we still can't stop the devastation it brings; we can only mitigate it to some extent. Think back to the widespread loss of life in the tidal wave that swept through parts of Southeast Asia in late 2004. Close to a quarter of a million people lost their lives, including a few people thousands of miles away in South Africa.

How much more daunting would the sea be for someone who lived thousands of years ago? Their perception, understanding, and experience of something like the vast oceans and wild seas naturally took on additional symbolic meaning that reflected their danger and power. Ancient people often regarded the sea as something supernaturally fearful, so when the ancients wrote about the sea, they commonly used it as a symbol for chaotic, destructive, and evil forces. These are the very forces God must conquer for the sake of order, goodness, and human existence.[174]

In the cosmogonic myths of ancient cultures, the supremacy of God (or the supremacy of one particular god out of the many gods they worshipped in a particular pantheon) was demonstrated when a deity conquered the evil chaos that was represented by the seas. In ancient China, the creation myth started with chaos. Chaos was repeatedly divided into measured sections,[175] which represents the establishment of order. The Babylonian myth of creation, the *Enûma Eliš*, talks very specifically about the battle between a god and the forces of chaos, with the god earning victory and subjugating the symbol for chaos.[176] Any deity's establishment of controlling boundaries for the oceans (creating land to hold back the chaos-sea) exemplifies this same symbolic pattern. Think of the contrast between a raging ocean and the tall, formidable cliff that blocks the waves. The ocean represents formless chaos (the absence of order), but the immovable, unchanging cliff represents the manifestation of absolute order. The waves will crash against it but fall back on themselves. The cliff remains unmoved and unchanging. In general, most of the creation myths of the ancient societies taught that the supreme deity formed some sort of physical order (land) among the chaos (sea). All of the creation stories from this general time period in this part of the world are strikingly similar with regard to this symbolic pattern. Creation myths relating to deities conquering symbols of chaos are common in Babylonian, Sumerian, Egyptian, and other cultures.[177]

The act of God (or the gods) to create order among chaos is fascinating, and it has deep meaning and relevance for a wide variety of religious and theological thought. Humanity cannot live with only the raging seas, but humanity can live on the land atop the cliff. The divine establishment of order among the chaos (of form as opposed to the absence of form) is what enabled human existence in the world. Hence, it is viewed not only as part of the greatest display of divine power (cosmogony), but it is also the primary display of divine goodness from the human perspective: it is this act that enables human life. Cosmogonic myths taught that without the establishment of order, we would not exist due to lack of a stable or fixed place.[178]

To see an example of its importance, we can look to Egypt. In the Egyptian Book of the Dead, Ra is considered the ascendant deity and is praised for replacing chaos with order. Other passages have an adherent invoking the need for his heart to know divine order, while yet one more passage talks about a man who loved divine order as opposed to sin.[179] These clearly show the alignment of order with goodness and chaos with evil. The exact phrase used, "[Ra] placed order in the place of chaos," represents creation of the first solid earth in the midst of the chaotic seas. It was known as the primeval mound.[180] It was significant enough to be used as justification for Ra's ascendant position in the Egyptian hierarchy of gods. It is also commemorated as part of Egypt's most identifiable symbol: the pyramid. The capstone (the final top piece) of an Egyptian pyramid is called the *Benben* stone. In Utterance 600 of the Pyramid Texts, we see it translated into English as the "Phoenix Stone," but the original text reads, "*uben en ek em beneben em hut ben em iunu*" (note the word from which we get "benben").[181] This stone represents the creation of the primordial mound (order), among the sea (chaos), which is a common pattern.[182]

The abstract concepts of order and chaos, symbolized by land among the sea, eventually morphed to personify the concept of evil/chaos/sea into something a bit more concrete: a sea beast (often a serpentine aquatic beast). Sometimes this aquatic beast was also represented by an amphibious beast that came up out of the sea and onto land.[183] Think of the giant sea monsters or sea serpents as examples. Canaanite myth had Baal conquering a chaotic beast known as "Prince Sea."[184] Mesopotamian creation myths also evolved from sea subjugation to the conquering of a personified sea beast named Tiamat.[185] This pattern of sea/chaos/evil/beast manifests in nearly all of the ancient mythologies, including in the Canaanite story of creation,[186] in ancient China,[187] and in Norse mythology, In the Norse variation, Thor battles Jörmungandr, who is a giant sea serpent.[188] While the Norse myths vary in the details, they share the same pattern of the deity fighting chaos as embodied in a serpentine sea creature.

Eventually people further refined that symbol of the sea beast into dragons, which were often very serpentine. For example, The Babylonians believed quite explicitly as creation being the victory of order over chaos, and the dragon of chaos was a personification of the chaotic deep water.[189] Snakes and serpents became common symbols of this theme as well. Illuujanka was the snake in the Hittite myth and Apop was the giant serpent the Egyptian sun god struggled with.[190] In a portion of Hindu scriptures dating to the approximate time of the captivity of the Israelites in Egypt, the Rigveda references the "serpent of the deep."[191] The use of "deep" in symbolism like this refers to the primeval, chaotic waters. The Greeks told of the serpentine basilisk with evil powers; it could kill with a look.[192] These symbols held the same core meaning (chaos/evil), but the aquatic component of the symbol dissipated over time.

Saint George conquering the dragon is an example of a popular myth that originated in ancient cosmogonies. I recall seeing references to St. George in various locations during my UK visits, including at Windsor castle. Originally the cultures from the Levant taught the standard subjugation of the chaos-seas, then it morphed to conquering a sea beast, then it changed to conquering a dragon. Eventually the real person of St. George was conflated with the stories of conquering evil by defeating a dragon. For example, some believe that the legend of St. George is really an adaption of the ancient Egyptian stories regarding Horus and Set.[193]

The particulars of the cosmogonic myth can change even though the pattern stays the same. One example stands out in this regard. The Ayta people living near Mt. Pinatubo in the Philippines relate a legend that stretches far back into their oral history. They told of the evil sea spirit named Bacobaco. Bacobaco was a huge turtle that breathed fire. In a battle with a good deity, this fire-breathing turtle tried to hide in the water, but he was unsuccessful. Eventually he took refuge in mountain, which then exploded ferociously and caused much destruction over the course of three days. This myth clearly shows the evil sea beast pattern, only this time using an aquatic animal the locals were familiar with. Instead of a fire-breathing dragon, they had a fire-breathing turtle. They associated an ancient, terrifying eruption of their local volcano with the cosmogonic pattern of an evil sea beast.[194]

Cosmogony in the Bible

Genesis offers our first glimpse of these same patterns. It refers to the chaos by the simple representation of the sea: "The earth was formless and void, and darkness was over the surface of the deep, and the Spirit of God was moving over the surface of the waters" (Genesis 1:2). The words used to represent "the deep" and "the waters" are similar to the language used in nearby cultures' tales of chaotic-evil bodies of water or sea beasts.[195] While some people believed the primordial chaos was a pre-existent, eternal thing God had to conquer before He could create, Genesis does not actually teach that. The Bible teaches that God alone is eternal; there was no pre-existing, co-eternal evil chaotic force. However, the Genesis tale does share some of the same pattern as all other cosmogonies: order instead of chaos. Technically nothingness is a pure form of chaos since total chaos is the absence of any order at all, and at least some small amount of order (form) is required for something to even exist in the first place. In that sense, the biblical doctrine of creation *ex nihilo* (out of nothing) is God's establishment of order in the complete and total absence of order (pure chaos).

Note that in the progression of events cited in Genesis, the sea was first. As previously discussed, humans can't live in the sea. In Genesis

1:6-10, the waters are made orderly and contained. This section culminates with these two key verses:

> Then God said, "Let the waters below the heavens be gathered into one place, and let the dry land appear"; and it was so. God called the dry land earth, and the gathering of the waters He called seas; and God saw that it was good (Genesis 1:9-10).

The waters were contained by the first dry land. This is similar to the myths we see in all the cultures of this area (think of the primeval mound). It was this definitive act of God that both created the world and made it habitable for humanity. This shows that not only did He create *ex nihilo*, but He also demonstrated his absolute divine power and authority by creating form among the formless. Note that this is followed by God's own pronouncement—for the first time—that this is "good." This again reinforces the symbolic pattern that the primary good relative to humanity is the creation of order among the chaos that allows for human life. Regardless of the form of expression used to represent the concept, it is widely agreed that the God of the Bible created the universe by imposing His will, order, and form on the emptiness and chaos.[196]

In other sections of the Bible we see further evidence of the patterns of cosmogonic thought. Sections of Job and Psalms refer to the mythical pattern of the conquering of the sea beast prior to the creation of humanity.[197] In Job we see the pattern of God conquering the sea beast named Rahab. "He quieted the sea with His power, And by His understanding He shattered Rahab" (Job 26:12). The psalmist used these same patterns when describing the waters, the sea beasts, and the order God established. "You divided the sea by Your strength; You broke the heads of the sea monsters in the waters. You crushed the heads of Leviathan . . . You have established all the boundaries of the earth" (Psalm 74:13-14a, 17a). We also see the prophet Isaiah making use of these cosmogonic symbols. "Was it not You who cut Rahab in pieces, Who pierced the dragon?" (Isaiah 51:9b)

These ancient modes of thought and symbolism also continued into the New Testament. For example, when John described the arrival of the beast in Revelation, he used an ancient, symbolic pattern when expressing the nature and origin of the beast as evil. "Then I saw a beast coming up out of the sea" (Revelation 13:1b). Many interpreters of Revelation have tried to use this passage as an indicator to help figure out the country of origin for the beast. However, in the context of the cultures of the Bible, this was a clear use of the chaos/sea/evil/beast pattern, and as such it was a declaration that the beast is pure evil (it may or may not have additional meaning beyond that). In Revelation 12 we see Satan described as "the dragon" (Revelation 12:3-4), which is a continuation of this pattern. Later, when John described the new heaven and the new earth, which are perfect and free from evil, he specifically wrote, "Then I saw a new heaven and a new earth; for the first heaven and the first earth passed away, and *there is no longer any sea*" (Revelation 21:1, emphasis added). The last phrase of the verse would seem very odd if not for our ability to gain understanding by adjusting our personal context to match the one held by the people of the Bible. When we do this, we understand the clear symbolic declaration that there will be no more evil and chaos. Even the *potential* for evil has been eliminated.

Appealing to Cosmogonic Powers

Despite differences in their religious beliefs, this cosmogonic mode of thought was widespread throughout the region where the early people of the Bible lived. Regardless of whether or not their beliefs were monotheistic, polytheistic, henotheistic, or otherwise, there is a universal and important concept to take away from the various cosmogonic myths: the supremacy of power required to create the world, and that only an ascendant or supreme deity had the power necessary to do it. To create the world, to develop it into a specific design to support human life, to conquer the chaos and establish the persistence of ordered form: this is something only God can do. As a result of the supreme, divine power required for creation, the ancient thought was that there must have been a tremendous amount of this divine power and energy present during creation. Whether that power was put to use to create an existence *ex nihilo*, or if it was put forth to subjugate the powerful seas, or even if it was harnessed and spent in the killing of a terrible, primeval monster, the early people believed that the power of the divine was on full display during that time before humanity.

It was precisely the ancient perception of an overabundance of divine, cosmogonic power that drove so many ancient religious practices to invoke the creation in some way. By aligning something with the creation, they could symbolically become contemporaneous with the creation and call upon or tap into the abundance of cosmogonic power.[198] For example, if the ancients needed a ritual associated with life (healing, birth, etc.), they would appeal to the powers present at the cosmogony by means of an imitation that might be a recital of the creation myth or a ritual re-enactment of the act of creation.[199] The recitation of the creation myth is probably the easiest form of cosmogonic imitation for us to understand, but we find other forms that were used in abundance throughout the ancient world.

Sometimes a specific symbol was used during a particular ritual. This might involve drawing a representation of the earth (imitation of creation) or by using a symbol that represented the whole earth. Using the cosmogonic symbol was one form of repeating the act of creation. If someone drew a symbol of the earth, then it was understood that he or she was projecting themselves back, in a metaphysical sense, to the mythical time of creation when the creative powers of life were on full display. The symbols of the earth often consisted of something that represented the four cardinal directions because in the minds of the ancient people, they thought of the universe as having a center point and stretching out in all directions, as best represented by the four cardinal directions (north, south, east, and west).[200] If a specific symbol represented the four cardinal directions, using it represented the whole of creation and qualified as a cosmogonic appeal. The ancients thought that this imitation of creation brought them closer to the time of supreme, divine power and helped them to win divine favor. They re-enacted this most sacred of times and stayed close to the power of the divine and the true reality it represented.[201] In the Bible, we see this concept represented inside the Temple of Solomon. The molten sea inside the temple was a giant, round container of water that probably held more than ten thousand gallons of water based on conservative estimates of ancient measures. The water was contained within a giant, bronze basin that was specifically mounted on top of twelve molten oxen. The oxen were in groups of three, and each group of three specifically faced one of the cardinal directions: north, west, south, and east (1 Kings 7:23-26). The massive water basin represented God's ordering of the universe by establishing boundaries for the seas. That it was set upon something representing the cardinal directions further emphasizes the cosmogonic nature of the symbol: it represents the full extent of creation. This is a clear cosmogonic symbol that celebrates God's power. Cosmogonic symbols and rituals might sound strange to a modern Christian; however, there is an example that is common among Christian churches. This ritual makes use of a cosmogonic symbol: baptism.

Baptism

Baptism makes use of two interactive elements regarding the believer and water: immersion and emersion. Immersion in water is equivalent to destruction or death.[202] Consider what happens if you drop an item into the water and you watch as it sinks. Even in the clearest of deep waters, as the item sinks it becomes more difficult to see. The visual clarity starts to fade as the light waves are refracted and the outline of the object starts to become wavy. It eventually fades from sight entirely. In symbolic religious thought, this is equivalent to regression from existence and form to non-existence and the lack of form. In other words, it is symbolic of death. On the other hand, emersion from water is equivalent to creation and life. [203] Using the same example, think of what happens as the object that sunk to the bottom now rises up toward the top and out of the water. The closer it gets to the surface, the more the form appears to solidify. It starts off difficult to see with little visual definition. As it rises, the light waves refract less, and the waviness in the form gives way to more structure. Eventually the item emerges from the water and you can see it with perfect clarity. In symbolic religious thought, this is analogous to creation. Remember the primeval mound from cosmogonic myth? This was the creation of order among chaos, or in a more concrete sense, the emergence of land from the sea. It's the same type of thinking. Remember that only the divine can perform this act of creation. That is important when considering baptism.

In the baptism ritual, the person is fully submerged into water.[204] This is symbolic of the death to self and to sin. The old form and the old self is broken up and fades away. When the person emerges from the water, this is symbolic of being a new creation in Christ. Remember that in cosmogonic myth, only the divine can make creation like that. Only God brings something new and solid out of the chaotic waters. So, when someone dies to self in baptism, it is God alone who is bringing a fresh creation up out of the water. Baptism symbolizes the believer being created completely new and only by God's divine work. No human role or effort is part of the creation symbolism of baptism. This is why I adore baptism as part of a believer's life. To me it's one of the most symbolically powerful things that takes place in the life of an individual.

Baptism is not the end of cosmogonic thought in religious practices. As we move into the next chapter, we'll see cosmogonic thought enter into some expressions of sacred space.

CHAPTER 13

Sacred Space

ON MY FATHER'S SIDE, THE Hein family came over to the United States from what used to be the town of Hillersdorf in the Austro-Hungarian Empire. They were devout members of the Evangelische Kirche, (in other words, they were Lutherans). In today's modern world, many things have changed. Hillersdorf is now called Holčovice, which on today's maps lies so far north and east in the Czech Republic, it's just a stone's throw from Poland. Some things change—a lot—but the Hein family is still largely Lutheran. My grandfather entered Concordia Seminary immediately after high school, and he served as a pastor in the Missouri Synod Lutheran Church his entire adult life, including churches in Missouri, Wisconsin, Iowa, Washington, British Columbia, Idaho, Oregon, and California. He eventually retired due to advanced age and the fact that he was no longer able to perform his duties as well as he thought a pastor should be able to. However, that didn't kill the spark of ministry within him. When I visited him recently, he had difficultly remembering me, my name, or even what our relationship is. However, despite these significant and growing memory issues, he still knows he is a Lutheran pastor, and he leads hymns and helps serve communion in their Lincoln City retirement community. On Sunday mornings, you could find him alongside my grandmother greeting people at the last church he pastored, St. Peter the Fisherman in Lincoln City, Oregon. Despite his difficulty in remembering who I was during our last visit, he constantly encouraged me to follow Jesus and be thankful to him in everything. Visiting Grandpa at his church was something I always looked forward to throughout my entire life.

When I was younger, I considered my grandfather's church building to be a very special place, perhaps in part because it was so different from the church buildings I grew up in. From the age of six to my current age, all of my home churches have been located in large auditoriums, converted gymnasiums, and even a former bowling alley. But the churches my grandfather pastored were far more traditional, and I knew there would always be a long, narrow sanctuary accented with stained glass and filled with pews. There would be an altar and a place up front to kneel when receiving communion or a blessing from the pastor. The service would be structured, solemn, and reverential, and afterward my grandfather would stand by the exit and personally greet every person in attendance. All of these things combined to make his churches truly feel like they occupied a special space, something set apart for the service and presence of God.

Since those days in my youth, I've visited a number of special, sacred buildings. Some, like St. Peter's Basilica in Rome or the Notre-Dame Cathedral in Paris, are famous, and deservedly so. Walking inside one feels transported to a place that is markedly different from the world just outside the doors, almost as if the holy building shares in a slightly different, elevated reality. When visiting the Duomo di Milano, the special feel of the interior of the huge cathedral carried through to the top of the structure. People exited the sanctuary proper and gathered on the roof of the cathedral in great numbers, enjoying the sun and the literal elevation above the mundane city surrounding it. The gothic pinnacles and spires both surrounded the visitors and drew their attention upward toward the sky. It was a unique and special experience.

But that sort of special feeling isn't just limited to the famous churches with exorbitant construction costs. Whether it is a giant European marvel, a small brick church in Idaho Falls, a tent revival in Puyallup, or the San José parish church in Tlaxcala, they all have the feel of being a special place of devotion. Every holy structure commemorates and marks sacred space for the inhabitants of that region who follows that faith. They are places where people focus on the awareness of the supernatural rather than being wholly focused on the ordinary world and mundane things.

Understanding Sacred Space

In general terms, sacred space is an area that is marked or consecrated as a holy area. From our earlier chapters, we have already seen the implication of the existence of sacred space. Stonehenge is an example of sacred space. It is a place of special spiritual significance to the people who created it. Any place with a hierophany was considered to be a sacred space consecrated as such by the hierophany. Think back to Jacob when he had his dream of the ladder, which was an obvious hierophany. When he awoke from his dream, he declared that the area he was in was God's house, and then he marked the area with a standing stone. He clearly recognized that that area participated in an elevated reality due to the divine manifesting in that space. He believed it was a persistent, ongoing sacred space, hence the need to mark it as such. But perhaps the most explicit example comes from Moses.

After he had fled from Egypt earlier in his life, he was out in the wilderness when he encountered the famous burning bush. The bush was not consumed by the flames, and God spoke to him from the burning bush. Among other things, God directly indicated that the area was sacred space. God said, "Do not come near here; remove your sandals from your feet, for the place on which you are standing is *holy ground*" (Exodus 3:5, emphasis added). Note that it is God who explicitly indicates the existence of sacred space. Furthermore, God indicated the need to act differently in that sacred space ("remove your sandals"). This also reinforces the notion that mundane human activity is not always acceptable inside of this sacred space or that a higher degree of respect needs to be shown. But it goes to illustrate that for religious people, not all places are mundane. Some places have a special spiritual or supernatural quality to them.[205]

There are more and less formal versions of sacred space. A good example of a less formal variation might be Moses before the burning bush. There was no indicator of the border of that particular sacred space. Moses did not see a border drawn upon the ground that indicated he was crossing over into a holy area. However, the hierophany in that location, and of course the explicit words of God, indicated that he was not on mundane, ordinary ground.

In religious behavior, there have been many ways of marking informal or transitory sacred space, such as marking the earth. For example, a cultist's drawn pentagram on the ground might indicate sacred space for rituals. Also, anything that symbolically represented the cosmogony indicated the appeal to the divine in that space. One of the common ways of representing the cosmogony was to represent the four cardinal directions. A representation or creation of something indicating north, south, east, and west was a representation of all of creation (either the earth or the whole universe). For example, Native American concepts include sacred circles that represent the four cardinal points while the 360 degrees of the circle symbolically represents the whole of creation.[206] The Wiradjuri and Kamilario, indigenous Australian tribes, make a circle on the ground for their ceremonies, which is a cosmogonic representation.[207] In the West African Vodun religion, which started approximately six thousand years ago and is the source of modern-day voodoo, they made use of a circle with crossing perpendicular lines in it. It used both the circle and the lines representing the four directions as an imitation of the cosmogony.[208] The Algonkian people along the Atlantic coast constructed a sacred building that represented the cosmogony. It was a rectangular building, and it had four doors, one on each side. The floor represented the earthly realm, the roof represented the upper realm, and the four walls represented the four horizons (or the four cardinal directions). It is a constructed re-actualization of the creation of the world.[209] The representation of the number four found in late Stone Age materials (such as etching on a mammoth tusk) in the Russian Plain represent the cosmogony as well.[210] This was a universal and ancient concept. By invoking the cosmogony, which was the most powerful demonstration of divine power in ancient thought, it was human invocation of divine power and connection.

A formal indicator of sacred space would often involve construction. We have already talked about the stone pillars or circles that were erected to mark sacred space. Going further, established places of worship are excellent examples of sacred space, and they had permanent, clearly established boundaries (usually the outer walls of the structure). All sacred spaces were centered around axis mundi, the connection between the realms, and the presence of the axis mundi effectively sanctified everything within the given boundaries of the construction. Hence, anyone who entered into the sacred building or room is participating in the presence of the axis mundi simply by being within the holy building. Temples provide us with the best ancient examples of formal sacred space. The entire space within the temple is effectively consecrated as a place of divine connection. For example, the world "temple" represented the "house of the god" while also being a building for sacred rites. In Egypt, the divine connection in the temple could be used for a king's consecration.[211] These sacred buildings effectively become a fixed, established center for religious living. Since the axis mundi is a point of orientation around which the ancient believer's life revolved, the structure representing sacred space provided him with a physical point of contact, something he could literally reach out and touch, that pointed to the non-physical, transcendent divine. This sacred building, constructed out of profane materials by profane humans, transcends its profane origin and becomes sacred in nature.

To people throughout the ages, the importance of the cosmogony cannot be overstated. The simple act of organizing something where there was previously an empty space, or simply bringing organization to a chaotic space, recalls the foundational concepts of the cosmogony. Organizing a space or constructing a building was a human imitation of the original creative work performed by the divine.[212] For example, J.R.R. Tolkien spoke of human sub-creation, which he exemplified when creating Middle-earth, the fantasy world central to his famous books. He created and organized something out of his own thoughts, although clearly his creation was nothing as significant as God's creation of the world. His human (sub)creation could be viewed as an act of worshiping God since Tolkien imitated God's great creation by creating.[213] Imitation of the divine can be an expression of belief and devotion. The phrase, "imitation is the sincerest form of flattery," holds true. It's similar to a child who imitates a parent because they want to be like their mom or dad.

My first parental experience of this was comical. When Ephraim was about eighteen months old, I spent a couple of weeks sitting on the couch recovering from surgery with an ice pack on the surgical site to reduce the pain and swelling. Ephraim grabbed an ice pack of his own, climbed up next to me on the couch, and placed the ice pack on himself with a huge smile on face. He wanted to be just like his papa, and he was so proud! Chris and I thought it was both hilarious and touching at the same time.

When it came to constructing sacred buildings, the builders often liked to mark or consecrate their building with cosmogonic symbolism.

Some sacred buildings specifically incorporate obvious cosmogonic symbolism in their construction. One example of cosmogonic construction was cited in the previous chapter. The molten sea in Solomon's temple was a cosmogonic symbol in a building that was clearly sacred space. The cosmogonic symbolism of the molten sea is clear. There was the sea (water of chaos), contained by form (the creation of land by God), placed on top of another cosmogonic symbol (the oxen facing the four cardinal directions). Not only was Solomon's temple sacred space, it was sacred space that invoked the cosmogonic symbol, which indicated the absolute supremacy and power of God. The ritual cleansing basins used by priests in the temple followed cosmogonic symbolism as hands were washed (purified and made holy, like a baptism of the hands) before many of the priestly duties were performed.

The tabernacle and the temple both contained an internal area that was even more sacred than the outer areas. The Holy of Holies was where the Ark of the Covenant was located, and the presence of God would manifest inside the Holy of Holies. When the tabernacle was first dedicated, God spoke audibly to Moses from within the Holy of Holies, which is another clear example of a hierophany and sacred space (Exodus 7:89-8:19). In fact, some rabbinic writers taught that Israel itself was a holy space that became more and more holy the closer you were to the spiritual center. The country borders were holy, then when you got closer to Jerusalem that space became more holy, then the city itself in various degrees all the way down to the most holy space, the Holy of Holies. [214]

Sacred Construction from Ancient Times to Modern Times

Moving through time to more recent examples, many buildings have been constructed using the invocation of sacred space or imitation of the cosmogony, even for "ordinary" buildings. This was done to invoke the recognition, blessing, or approval of the divine. Recalling that construction itself is a form of sub-creation, which is an imitation of the divine creation, cosmogonic symbology was incorporated into the buildings themselves or as a ritual when starting construction.

The idea of the cornerstone is an example of this. Cornerstones in construction have been used since biblical times. A cornerstone was a cosmogonic symbol used at the start of construction. The placing of this first stone was a ritual that imitated the establishment of order (land) among chaos (the seas). In an empty building plot, establishing the cornerstone was symbolic of the primeval mound, and it was the reference point for all the construction and activity that followed. The ancient Assyrians, during the reign of King Assurbanipal, left instructions for a three-day cornerstone ritual that involved priests and magicians. More than 2,500 years later, the University of Chicago used the instructions found on the ancient clay tablets to re-enact this ritual when starting construction on a new academic building.[215] In the Bible, the prophet Isaiah referred to the cornerstone that people should believe in (Isaiah 28:16). Both Peter and Paul later refer to Jesus as the cornerstone (1 Peter 2:6, Ephesians 2:20).

In some construction in India, the cosmogony was symbolized in a more direct form as the defeat of the chaotic sea monster was re-actualized at the start of construction. An astronomer (someone who references the upper realm for direction) would indicate where the cornerstone should be placed. The chief mason would then drive a stake into the ground at that location, because the head of the chaotic snake was believed to lie beneath that point. Driving the stake into the snake's head in the ground fixed an exact location among the chaos it represented, and then the cornerstone was laid on that location.[216] By symbolically killing the snake, the primordial chaos that threatened established form was subjugated, and a stone (representing form and the absolute) was laid as the primary building piece and point of reference for further construction. By engaging in cosmogonic imitation, they were appealing to the power of the divine that was present at the time of creation in an attempt to ensure longevity in construction and in life.

Sometimes the builders included cosmogonic symbolism in the structure of the building as a whole. For example, in Waropen, New Guinea, a specific building for the men was built at the center of the village. Their beliefs taught that the four walls corresponded to the four directions (cosmogonic symbolism), and the ceiling represented the upper realm.[217] Some long houses of the Sioux were similar. They had four walls, each containing a window that looked out in one of the four directions, and each wall was painted a different color. This was done to indicate the four cardinal directions and invoke the cosmogony as part of the construction of the building.[218] In the medieval Hindu capital of Vijayanangare, various sacred shrines are oriented according to the cardinal directions.[219] Mesoamerican architecture indicated sacred space where the supernatural realm met human reality.[220]

Modern Christians should be able to grasp the experience of sacred space on some level. Many Christians treat the actual church building as something just a bit more special than something more ordinary, such as the local convenience store. It's common for people to be a bit more reserved when in a church building. There are some activities or conversations they might have at a barbecue or sports event that they might not have in a church. Of course, the grander the construction of the church, the more experiential impact it might have. The Sistine Chapel in Vatican City, for example, may provide the believer with a greater sense of grandeur than a small, dilapidated church in some remote wilderness region. Personally, I found St. Peter's to be the most impressive church or cathedral I have ever set foot in. When Chris and I went in there, we spoke in hushed tones, despite the presence of very few people around us. It was a large space that drew the eyes upward toward the heavens, and it felt like a special, sacred place. Many cathedrals have rules regarding attire. For example, visitors may need to wear something on their head, women may need to ensure their shoulders are covered, knees must not be exposed, or open-toed shoes may not be allowed.

True Sacred Space Centers on God

Sacred space always implies an axis mundi present in that location; there is a connection with the divine in that area. For example, the church is a space where believers gather to worship, learn, and hear God's word delivered through one of His servants. Being at church is about connection with God and orienting one's life on God, as well as connection with those that have a similar focus. For the Christian, not every space deemed to be sacred by various people is actually acceptable to God. A space dedicated to Krishna might indeed be a place of supernatural presence, but it would not be a place of God's presence. Indeed, the Christian does not want to encounter a supernatural presence at a place like that since it is probably something else as alluded to in Paul's letter to Timothy: "deceitful spirits and doctrines of demons" (1 Timothy 4:1b). Only those sacred spaces which glorify the true God would be considered biblically acceptable. Furthermore, the acceptability of any sacred space continues only so long as it is God who is glorified and valued by believers, not the actual geometric space or the building itself. In the end, it is the same today as it was in the beginning: it is always all about God.

CHAPTER 14

The Center

IT HAD BEEN A LONG couple of days of sightseeing in Alsace, and I was exhausted. At this point, Dan, Juli, Chris, and I were in the town of Colmar (in eastern France) looking for a place to dine. The previous evening, on our way out of Colmar and back to our villa in Rouffach, we noticed a specific restaurant and decided to come back and dine there. So, in the late afternoon of the next day, Dan took over driving and I moved to the backseat to sit with my wife. It had been a long couple of days, and soon I fell into a deep sleep. I woke up briefly, just long enough to notice it was now dusk. The next thing I knew, I woke up again, and it was clearly night. At this point we were in a residential part of town, and we were lost. I mumbled some advice (which I don't think anyone heard), and then I feel asleep again. This pattern repeated itself over the course of about two hours. I kept waking up, noticing we were lost, giving advice on how to get un-lost, and then I'd fall back asleep.

Now I should point out that being lost, even though I wasn't driving, was primarily my fault. This was Dan and Juli's first trip to Europe. Dan wanted to rent a GPS, and I told him that based on my experience, it really wasn't necessary. Driving on back roads and seeing unexpected sights was a pleasure, and it was easy to find your way from town to town. This much is usually true. But I didn't account for actually trying to get around inside of a city, and that can be a real nightmare. Let me say now for all the world to read: it was a bad call on my part.

Finally, I woke up for real, and we were still lost. They had been driving around for the better part of two hours. This time I spoke up a bit louder, and probably with some exasperation as I repeated what I had been mumbling earlier: "Just go to the center." It's "centre-ville" in French or "Zentrum" in German. Those are the magic words that can get you un-lost in a heartbeat. It seems like most European towns clearly mark their city center, which is usually the older, scenic, and historical part of town (and a magnet for tourists). And since they're in the cultural center of the city (if not always the exact geographic center), there are usually major roads leading either directly into the center or to a ring of roads surrounding it. If you go to the center, it's much easier to orient yourself and figure out where to go from there.

At this point, I saw a sign for "Gare de Colmar" (the central train station). I exclaimed that we should follow the signs there since it would be in or near the city center, and we would easily find our way back once we reached the center. So, we did, and moments later we pulled up to the train station, which was near the center of town. And sure enough, the train station was actually sitting on the road to Rouffach itself. After two hours of being lost, it took less than five minutes to figure out where we were and reach our destination at the restaurant. All we had to do was rely on the center.

Symbols of the Center

There is one overwhelming, universal theme that stands out from the concepts of various hierophanies, axis mundi, and sacred spaces: the existence of an absolute center. All manifestations of the sacred indicate an external, transcendent absolute, which is what people use as a point of reference. However, it is more than just any ordinary point of reference, it is *the* point of reference from which all meaning should be derived. The center is the place of the sacred. It is the place in our profane existence where the divine makes a point of connection. It is where transcendent reality is manifested and made knowable for ordinary people. For a religious person, the transcendent reality is the absolute, true reality that helps us to live and gain orientation in our constantly shifting and unpredictable world.[221]

The prevalence of sacred space, hierophanies, and axis mundi demonstrate the desire for people to live in perpetual contact with the divine, in relation to the absolute reality that can guide their lives. The hierophany reveals an ongoing break in planes that allows connection with the divine. The physical, profane, geometric area of space where the break between planes occurs is a geographic center of sorts. We have seen the various ways people mark these places (stones, tree, mountains, temples, etc.). However, the fact that people mark a geographic center is simply the natural result of the fact that humans are finite, physical creatures that exist in a physical, profane realm. The geographic delineation is a profane construct that points to the divine reality of a sacred center. The true, sacred center is of the metaphysical variety, and the physical, geographic center simply represents it.

By the physical attempt to stay close to the geographic center, the ancient person was attempting to encourage and maintain metaphysical relevance in his or her life. After looking at the universal, underlying forms of ancient religious experience, it is abundantly clear that religious people have always tried to live as near as possible to this sacred center.[222] Lacking a clear and highly developed theological language, the ancient people represented these concepts of the center through the use of myths, symbols, and rituals.

The early people of the Bible were part of a wider culture that was immersed in these mythical and symbolic thought patterns. When we read the Bible, we must remember that the context for understanding is not our modern context today. God's inerrant, inspired[223] word was given through ancient people who lived and wrote in the context of their lives, not ours. As such, if we seek a full understanding of the Bible, we have to recognize that their ancient thinking could not be separated from myth and symbol.[224] However, as pointed out earlier, use of terms such as "myth" and "symbol" do not imply a lack of literal truth. There are mythical types and episodes found in the Bible that are literally true even though they make use of mythical and symbolic patterns. It is important to remember that Jesus became manifest in the profane world, and in doing so brought confirmation of supernatural reality and absolute divine reality in our profane world. His incarnation took place in our physical, human time line. This is a revelation of God in human history, and as such, it validates the specific symbols and myths in the Bible that point to God as true.[225]

God Is the Center

All of the human conceptions of the experience of the sacred point to the divine as being the true center of existence. For the Christian that center is God. It is never the standing stone, the cosmic tree, a holy mountain, a sacred staff, or the church building. God is always the true center.

Some could argue that central, divine sacrality has been lost in modern Christian culture. For many people who profess Christianity, it would be telling to observe if they actually value and place God on the throne of absolute truth and make Him the center point of their lives. A quick survey of the Christian colleges would reveal many professors who teach their students relative truth (neo-orthodoxy) as opposed to the absolute and unchanging truth that God reveals. The absolute guide becomes a relative guide based on ever-shifting cultural norms and political pressures. For many people, the true center is replaced by a Sunday morning routine, which is quickly discarded when "real life" begins on Monday.

However, for the ancient Hebrews, the divine was taught and lived as truly central. At no point could one consider the ancient people to be irreligious, as one might claim of modern man. The spiritual challenges that Israel faced in the Bible were not challenges generated by a displacement of the concept of sacrality from the central role, but rather it was the displacement of God from that central role. Ritual and pattern became more important than God. Often this manifested in clear idolatry. The myths, symbols, and rituals that God used to teach people became the center point of their lives instead of God Himself. The temple, prophet, sacred space, or God-given rule could be confused as holy and worthy of worship itself instead of focusing on the divine it pointed to.[226] When Moses instructed the people not to engage in idolatry, the purpose was to keep God at the center instead of something else that could subtly displace Him in the hearts of the Israelites. In the life of the Israelites, the religious reforms and ever-increasing rules were a reaction to the confusion of ordinary people who paid more attention to signs and symbols than to God.[227] It was not the staff of Moses, the Ark of the Covenant, or the physical tabernacle that were themselves holy and worthy of adoration and sacrifice; rather, it was the presence of God that was holy. The items that were consecrated as holy or the rules that indicated holiness in living were not, and never will be, equivalent in value to that which is intrinsically and eternally holy from before the creation of the universe.

True worship and understanding of the divine means having God in your life as the absolute center. Idolatry is when God is not the absolute center of your life. Note this definition is slightly different from the common thought that idolatry is only defined as having a different deity as the center. For example, the ancient Israelite worship of Baal is an example of clear idolatry. Their center of worship was not God;

they worshipped a different deity that was probably a demon or fallen angelic creature. But while people may *acknowledge* God intellectually as being the only center, *living* as if God is a relative center, one that is only acknowledged as important in certain aspects or times of life as determined by one's own opinion, is simply the elevation of oneself or one's own priorities to the place of the absolute center. This is also idolatry as one's own opinions become the center by which life is oriented. In this way, it is nothing more than a human's hopeless attempt to actualize the serpent's lie: "you will be like God" (Genesis 3:5b).

One of the great messages of Christianity is the precise message that God is the center of *all* meaning, purpose, and life. In fact, He is the center of the entire universe since it exists to glorify God.[228] As humans are personal creations, God is the personal creator from which our personhood comes. This is one of the key failures of Eastern or philosophical pantheism: that an impersonal reality could emanate or manifest personhood.

We serve a God who does not remain at a safe distance while worrying about His own honor. We center on a God who shared our distress and affliction when He became incarnate. We are not dealing with an unapproachable deity but with a God who has a human face and who is not indifferent to us, but rather He is deeply involved with us in our need.[229] We do not serve a God "who cannot sympathize with our weaknesses, but One who has been tempted in all things as we are, yet without sin" (Hebrews 4:15).

With regard to Christ's instruction to live meekly, one writer observed that it means that we are to live a lifestyle that does not rely on our own power, but rather to live a life centered on God and on His power.[230] Saint Thomas Aquinas referred to the absolute center for human living when he wrote that our main goal is to enjoy God (not the symbols of Him), and that our aims in life are only real in a spiritual sense when we have Him at the center. Our goals are not legitimate when they direct us away from having Him at the center.[231]

Jesus Is the Center

As God incarnate in the profane plane, Jesus is the center. Given the existence of true religious symbols and forms in the Bible, it should be no surprise that Christ fulfilled the mythical forms and archetypes created by God that point to Himself. After all, Jesus explicitly claimed divinity. In John 8:58, he claimed to be "I Am," the name of God referenced in Exodus 3:14. In verse 19 he made it clear that if people knew him (Jesus), they would know God. In verse 23 he spoke to the religious leaders around him and said, "You are from below, I am from above; you are of this world, I am not of this world." These are all claims of divinity and they match the patterns of religious thought understood by the people of that time. That is why the religious leaders of the time sought to kill him for blasphemy; they knew he was claiming absolute divinity.

But there are two more examples we should look at. Most people are familiar with these two stories, but many also miss the significance of them. In Matthew 14:22-33, we see the story of Jesus walking on the water. Remember that only the ascendant divine was able to tame the waters. When Jesus walks on the waters, he is demonstrating a type of power that speaks to his divinity. And when Peter is focused on Jesus, then God supports him in walking on the water. When he loses his focus, he sinks. We see another powerful example from a different story.

On that day, when evening came, He said to them, "Let us go over to the other side." Leaving the crowd, they took Him along with them in the boat, just as He was; and other boats were with Him. And there arose a fierce gale of wind, and the waves were breaking over the boat so much that the boat was already filling up. Jesus Himself was in the stern, asleep on the cushion; and they woke Him and said to Him,

"Teacher, do You not care that we are perishing?" And He got up and rebuked the wind and said to the sea, "Hush, be still." And the wind died down and it became perfectly calm. And He said to them, "Why are you afraid? Do you still have no faith?" They became very much afraid and said to one another, "Who then is this, that even the wind and the sea obey Him?" (Mark 4:35-41)

The cultural context of the disciples taught that no one except God could bring order to the chaos; only God could conquer the chaotic, destructive seas. It was God who had calmed the primeval waters. It was God who parted both the Red Sea and the Jordan River. And Jesus had just subjugated the sea using a few mere words. There was no more powerful symbol that could have been given to them at that time than the cosmogonic symbol of absolute divinity. Some modern critics have tried to discount the Bible by writing that Jesus never actually claimed to be God and that he only claimed to be a messenger from God. However, *they simply don't know what they are talking about.* Jesus both explicitly claimed and physically demonstrated divinity in the language and cultural context of that day. Any claim to the contrary is laughable.

By claiming to be God, Jesus was claiming to be the ultimate hierophany—by far the most important and real hierophany that humanity has ever experienced. No subsequent hierophany will ever surpass Christ in the flesh. There is no greater hierophany than God manifesting in physical, personal form to physically interact with the people of His creation. Remember the nature of a hierophany: the source of absolute truth for life and a point of connection with the divine. This describes Jesus perfectly, because that's what Jesus is.

Jesus taught people how to live (the absolute, central guide for life). He said, "I am the way, and the truth, and the life" (John 14:6b), and he told people to "keep my commandments" (John 14:15b). Furthermore, he claimed to be the fulfillment of the law (the way to live) given to the Israelites by Moses. "Do not think that I came to abolish the Law or the Prophets; I did not come to abolish but to fulfill" (Matthew 5:17). When asked by a Sadducee which of the commandments was the most important, he replied with a response that put God (and therefore himself) at the center. "You shall love the Lord your God with all your heart, and with all your soul, and with all your mind" (Matthew 22:37b). He clearly claimed to be the absolute authority on how humans should live, which is one of the two primary functions of a hierophany.

The second aspect of a hierophany is the implied connection with the divine (the axis mundi). As Christ is God incarnate, it is obvious that anyone who has a connection with Christ has a connection with the divine. In a powerful validation of the spiritual concept of the axis mundi, Jesus said to Nathanael, "Truly, truly I say to you, you will see the heavens opened and the angels of God ascending and descending on the Son of Man [Jesus]" (John 1:51). This is a direct reference to the vision of Jacob at Haran where he saw the ladder (an axis mundi) connecting heaven and earth. In Jacob's vision the angels were ascending to heaven and descending to earth on the ladder (Genesis 28:10-19). In this passage from John, Jesus openly proclaims that he is this connection to heaven. As already demonstrated, the point of divine connection is the center for a believer; therefore, Jesus is claiming to be the center.

Furthermore, Paul admonished believers in 2 Corinthians 13:5, "Do you not recognize this about yourselves, that Jesus Christ is in you?" In his letter to the Galatians, he also wrote, "Christ lives in me" (Galatians 2:20). He wrote these things because when the believer accepts Jesus, Jesus *resides in them*. This is a form of language that indicates the Christian believer is sanctified as sacred space—as a place of connection with God because the ultimate hierophany is part of each believer. Note this does not impart any hint of divinity to the believer; it simply indicates that which is truly divine lives in and sanctifies the authentic believer. Going further with this concept, Paul also described, "The Holy Spirit who dwells in us" (2 Timothy 1:14). He also made the explicit declaration of the believer as sanctified sacred space when he wrote, "Do you not know that you are a temple of God and that the Spirit of God dwells in you? If any man destroys the temple of God, God will destroy him, for the temple of God is holy, and that is what you are" (1 Corinthians 3:16-17). Remember the temple is a place of sacred connection with the divine; if a believer is a temple, then the believer has a connection to God at all times and places. This doesn't make the believer the center, but it does mean the believer has 24-7 access to the real center: God. This is one of the wonderfully unique things about Christianity. Jesus has enabled authentic, divine connection for all of his followers, regardless of location or time. How is the connection made through Christ? It is made through his sacrifice and resurrection.

All of the elements of the supreme axis mundi are in place when Christ is crucified. He is crucified on a high hill (reaching toward the heavens), which is also a place of death called "the Place of a Skull" (John 19:17b). So, it is simultaneously a high hill, a place of death (representing the underworld), and a place existing in the middle (earthly) realm. He was crucified on a cross in the center of two other people. The cross is a wooden axis mundi (think back to the chapter on poles) that stretches from its base in the realm of the dead (Golgotha), through the human realm, and finally up toward the heavens. Many religious texts refer to the Cross of Christ as a ladder, column, or mountain.[232]

Furthermore, as a wooden (vegetative) axis mundi, the cross has the same characteristic as a cosmic tree (the potential for the renewal or sustaining of life). The apostles themselves recognized the cross as a tree when they spoke of "Jesus whom you murdered by hanging *on a tree*" (emphasis added, Acts 5:30b). The ESV translation of Peter's letter describes it similarly. "He himself bore our sins in his body on the tree, that we might die to sin and live to righteousness." The cross is the second biblical example of a cosmic tree, and it is juxtaposed with another tree from the Bible. Adam and Eve took living fruit off a living tree, and they died. Jesus is put back up on a dead tree to die, so that Adam and his descendants can live. Also, the shape of the cross itself is a cosmogonic symbol, which was earlier demonstrated to be indicative of a center. The intersecting lines indicating the cardinal directions clearly mark it as such. It is abundantly clear that Jesus is presented as the axis mundi. He is the center for human life.

By the sacrifice of Christ, the tragedy of the Fall—the pain and spiritual consequences of your sin—is replaced with hope and promise. God Himself has come to earth. He has made the way for people to connect with the divine, and He has given each one of us the central point of reference for life. Golgotha becomes a wonderful paradox: a place of death and of new life, a place where the broken connection is restored through the voluntary death of the source of life—who then lives again to offer the promise of true life to all who would follow. Dietrich Bonhoeffer, a brilliant pastor who was executed by the Third Reich for resisting the evil of the Nazi regime, sums it up well.

> The stem of the Cross becomes the staff of life, and in the midst of the world life is set up anew upon the cursed ground. In the middle of the world the spring of life wells up on the wood of the cross and those who thirst for life are called to this water, and those who have eaten of the wood of this life shall never hunger and thirst again. What a strange paradise is this hill of Golgotha, this Cross, this blood, this broken body! What a strange tree of life, this tree on which God himself must suffer and die—but it is in fact the Kingdom of Life and of the Resurrection given again by God in grace; it is the opened door of imperishable hope, of waiting, and of patience. The tree of life, the Cross of Christ, the middle of the fallen and preserved world of God, for us that is the end of the story of paradise.[233]

CHAPTER 15

Centralization and Decentralization

TALL, BROWN TREE TRUNKS STRETCHED high into the sky where they gave birth to a lush, emerald-green canopy. While the bright, Caribbean sun was brutally hot, the elevated foliage that protected us made the air temperature just perfect, so long as we stayed underneath the boundaries of its cover. Lush, delicious fruit grew in the area, providing both a delicious and refreshing treat. While Chris watched from the top of the gorge, Ephraim and I went down to the shore of the small, gentle river. Its clear waters moved easily over the smooth stones and created a soft, natural melody that provided the perfect backdrop for this peaceful garden-like area. A beautiful waterfall poured off of a cliff above us, which created a calm pool at its base. The water temperature was ideal, and Ephraim enjoyed himself as he swam in the middle of this amazing paradise. I sat on a nearby rock and took in the serenity of the area. Sunbeams of soft, filtered light came down from above and added a nice touch, particularly when they crossed with the light spray coming off of the waterfall and refracted into miniature rainbows. This was a natural area of amazing peace and beauty, unaltered by human hands. This was God's creation at its finest.

Eventually we had to leave the wonders of the deep jungle and return to our vacation residence. As we left the middle of the island and made our way toward the pier, more and more buildings came into view. The pristine jungle eventually gave way to full-blown civilization. The reality began to set in as our guide shared rumors of government corruption and the frustration of the local population. We witnessed leftover devastation from the effects of the last hurricane and heard the stories of the struggle to survive and recover. Returning to the main town, we were surrounded by markets, restaurants, and coffee shops—the typical trappings found in every town—but those weren't the reason we came to visit Dominica. No shopping, food, or music could compare with what we had experienced in the center of the island. And even once we returned to the luxury of the floating city we called home during that vacation, we were already reminiscing fondly about our time in that gorgeous, paradisiacal center. That center was where we wanted to be.

The Garden of Eden

In order to understand the fullness of the ancient myths, symbols, and rituals, as well as what they mean for modern Christians, it is necessary to return to something referenced only slightly in previous chapters: the start of human history. As this work is done from the perspective of Christian theism, the start of human history is the story of creation found in the first few chapters of Genesis. Regardless of if you think humans were created specially a few thousand years ago or if you think creation was a longer process guided by God as part of His divine sovereignty, the story of Adam and Eve teaches about the origin of humanity's existential state: broken connection with God.

The stories of creation, the Garden of Eden, and the Fall of man are the first myths related in the Bible. Remembering that ancient people did not have complex, theological language at their disposal, it not surprising that these early stories are flush with symbols and mythical archetypes.

Myths and symbols can accurately represent the transcendent truth claims of ancient people while being literally true at the same time. The thought of primitive people was expressed primarily through symbolic modes of communication.[234] How else could early people communicate the mysteries of the time before the Fall, which was filled with wondrous, divine experiences?

It is precisely these ancient stories, told using symbolic and mythical structure, that communicate metaphysical truth and provide the framework upon which Christian theology is developed. Our analysis of the story of creation starts in Genesis 2. In this part of the story, humanity is created, placed in the garden, and the Garden is described. The residents are also given one specific behavioral prohibition that they must obey, for their own sake.

This is the account of the heavens and the earth when they were created, in the day that the LORD God made earth and heaven. Now no shrub of the field was yet in the earth, and no plant of the field had yet sprouted, for the LORD God had not sent rain upon the earth, and there was no man to cultivate the ground. But a mist used to rise from the earth and water the whole surface of the ground. Then the LORD God formed man of dust from the ground, and breathed into his nostrils the breath of life; and man became a living being. The LORD God planted a garden toward the east, in Eden; and there He placed the man whom He had formed. Out of the ground the LORD God caused to grow every tree that is pleasing to the sight and good for food; the tree of life also in the midst of the garden, and the tree of the knowledge of good and evil. Now a river flowed out of Eden to water the garden; and from there it divided and became four rivers . . . The LORD God commanded the man, saying, "From any tree of the garden you may eat freely; but from the tree of the knowledge of good and evil you shall not eat, for in the day that you eat from it you will surely die" (Genesis 2:4-10, 16-17).

The Garden is a symbolic center. Centers always represent the place of communication with the divine. God was in the Garden, and God communed with Adam in the Garden. The separation had not yet occurred. The Garden was the archetype of the center. Real connection and communication existed in that place at that time. It was the original, archetypical sacred connection, in the original sacred space, in the original sacred time. However, symbols still existed in the Garden, particularly symbols of the center.

As described earlier in this work, the ancients believed that life comes from the center, which is the divine. In the center of the Garden stands the Tree of Life. The center is always representative of connection to God, who is the source of life, and the Tree of Life illustrates this wonderfully. Adam was not forbidden to eat from the Tree of Life; he could enjoy its fruit anytime he wanted. The tree was right there in the middle of the garden and represented the symbol of life when connected with God. As long as Adam stayed connected to the center, he had life (both spiritual and physical life). The Tree of Life is a symbol of connection to God. For the Christian, it is the origin of the ancient idea of the tree as an axis mundi. Afterward, the mythical form of the cosmic tree would later spread and become a common symbol in religious thinking.

Also pay attention to the river running through the Garden. Verses five and six indicate that it had not yet rained, but that the earth was watered via a mist that used to rise from the earth. In fact, the "*whole* surface of the ground" (emphasis added, Genesis 6b) was watered via this mist. While the river running through the Garden of Eden must have provided some form of hydration for the vegetation living next to it, it was not necessary for hydration since the rising mist provided all that was necessary. However, as soon as the river exited the garden it immediately split into four rivers. "Now a river flowed out of Eden to water the garden; and from there it divided and became four rivers" (Genesis 2:10). Remember what the number four represents in ancient thought? Anything representing four directions (such as four lines that gather together in one place) is a cosmogonic symbol that represents the world. This means the Garden is the center of the world, at least religiously; it is a cosmogonic symbol.[235] The cosmogonic symbol not only marks Eden as the center, it marks Eden as symbolically representing the whole of creation. The lesson of Eden as a cosmogonic symbol is, "What happens in Eden affects the world."

Finally, there are verses that appear to indicate the Garden may have been a place of higher elevation. For example, a river coming out of the garden indicates a higher elevation than the surrounding land. Plus, Ezekiel 28:11-14 talks of Satan's time in the Garden, which appears to be equated to the "holy mountain of God" in this passage. Also, the typical meeting place between the divine and humans was on mountaintops, as shown earlier in this book. There are many more complexities to this argument, which Michael Heiser laid out in more detail than we can go into here.[236] So we have God, the sacred Tree of Life, the cosmogonic rivers, and a meeting place with the divine that was probably in an elevated piece of land. Is there any doubt that these communicated symbols of the center—and the literal center—to the people of the Bible?

While there is an abundance of archetypical symbolism in the Garden, it does not appear that the symbolism was necessary for Adam. After all, he actually lived the life of sacred connection, in the sacred space, in what is essentially a sacred time. He did not necessarily need symbols to understand something that he actually lived every moment of his existence. Could Adam even truly conceive of what life would be like outside that? I don't think so. By definition, Adam lived a centered life. He lived in perfect communion and connection with the divine.

To say that Adam lived a centered life is to say that Adam lived a life that was entirely centered on God. Experientially, ideologically, spiritually—in all ways—God was the center of Adam's life. Adam was not the center; the world did not revolve around him even though he had been given a special role in it. He oriented his life on God and did not attempt to live otherwise or grasp divinity for himself.[237] Adam had life and connection with God because he voluntary centered his life on God. Part of this voluntary centering was displayed by his obedience to the single prohibition that he had been given.

The timing of the existence of the symbols is important: these symbols existed before they were needed. Adam did not need symbols in order to understand the concepts of sacrality, the center, or divine connection. He did not need them because he was actually experiencing them every day. The symbols are only needed when that direct experience is lost. God is the one who created the Tree, the rivers, the mountain, and the Garden. God created them because He knew they would be needed, and God created not only the physical symbolic patterns, but also the underlying truth as well. After Adam was cast out of the Garden, the symbols of the center became extremely important. Having lost all the immediate, personal, and perpetual experiences of sacrality, Adam had only the symbols by which to effectively communicate the theological truth of the Fall. No theological verbiage yet existed for him to rely upon.

It was through Adam's mythological story, saturated with pictures and symbols, that the knowledge and understanding of the Fall was passed on through the generations that would follow. Minds that were unconditioned for deep philosophical and theological thought were penetrated by the effectiveness of the story.

Decentralization and the Fall

Now the serpent was more crafty than any beast of the field which the LORD God had made. And he said to the woman, "Indeed, has God said, 'You shall not eat from any tree of the garden'?" The woman said to the serpent, "From the fruit of the trees of the garden we may eat; but from the fruit of the tree which is in the middle of the garden,

God has said, 'You shall not eat from it or touch it, or you will die.'"
The serpent said to the woman, "You surely will not die! For God
knows that in the day you eat from it your eyes will be opened, and
you will be like God, knowing good and evil." When the woman saw
that the tree was good for food, and that it was a delight to the eyes,
and that the tree was desirable to make one wise, she took from its
fruit and ate; and she gave also to her husband with her, and he ate
(Genesis 3:1-6).

Referring back to Genesis 2:17, Adam had only one prohibition:
not to eat from the Tree of the Knowledge of Good and Evil. He did
it anyway. The physical act of ingesting the produce from the Tree of
the Knowledge of Good and Evil is the point when the famous Fall
occurs and things turn bad. However, Adam's physical act of eating the
forbidden fruit was only the manifestation of a deeper, subtler internal
change. Eating the fruit was a just symptom of something else: Adam
removed God from the center of his life.

If at that specific moment, God was truly the center of Adam's
life, Adam would not have disobeyed God. Adam knew God to be the
source of life. Adam knew God to be the absolute. Adam lived a life
in connection with God and according to His will. Adam oriented his
entire life according to his relationship with God. However, for some
reason, which we will never know, at that specific moment Adam decided
that God was not the absolute center. When Adam chose to explicitly
disobey God, it was an outward manifestation of his internal decision
that God was not the absolute center of everything at all times.

The serpent indicated that God had lied to them about eating from
the Tree of the Knowledge of Good and Evil. In that moment, the serpent
communicated that God was not the source of truth or that He was not
the absolute, unchanging center. "The serpent said to the woman, 'You
surely will not die! For God knows that in the day you eat from it your
eyes will be opened, and you will be like God, knowing good and evil'"

(Genesis 3:4-5). Like any good lie, it was baited with truth. That they would know good and evil was not a lie. However, there was an explicit lie in the claim that they would not die. Further, there was an implicit lie in denying the truth and absolute centrality of God.

At some point, Adam made the decision to center his life on something or someone other than God. Perhaps he was centered on his wife, Eve. Perhaps he was centered on the serpent. Perhaps he was centered on himself. Modern people do this all the time. Anytime people place their own evaluations regarding what is true above God's explicit statements of truth, they have put themselves in the place of God. They have put themselves in center, in the place of absolute truth. They have attempted to "be like God," and in doing so they have lived the lie that leads to death. This holds true for modern people in so many ways. It's common for work or money to be the center of our lives. Activities we enjoy may be the true center of our decision making regarding how we live. Politics is a common replacement center. Even family, which is a great thing that should be a blessing from God, can replace God as the center in our lives. But just because it's common doesn't mean it's okay. As we see from Adam's example, the consequences are dire.

> Therefore the LORD God sent him out from the garden of Eden, to cultivate the ground from which he was taken. So He drove the man out; and at the east of the garden of Eden He stationed the cherubim and the flaming sword which turned every direction to guard the way to the tree of life" (Genesis 3:23-24).

Adam and Eve are cast out of the Garden, and the way back to the Tree of Life is barred. He no longer has access to the sacred tree from which he could eat freely and live. He can no longer be in the direct presence of God all the time in the original center of the world. He left the mountain garden and descended into what would be normal, mortal human life, with all of its trials and troubles.

I do not view this as terribly punitive, as an angry God who was looking to inflict as much suffering as possible on the disobedient humans. Rather, God had provided a sheltered, special place and taken Adam to be part of His special garden. Everything Adam needed was provided, and God enjoyed the special relationship with His human creation. This is what God desired, and this was how He deliberately set it up. Metaphorically speaking, God took Adam underneath His protective umbrella, but Adam made the decision to step out from underneath it. God simply let Adam know what the natural consequences were of living outside of the center and out from underneath the protective umbrella, as Adam chose to do when he decentralized God. Adam's decentralization precipitated the severance of the sacred connection, their expulsion from the sacred space, and the end of their sacred time in the Garden. Humanity's connection with God was changed.

CHAPTER 16:

Boundaries

WE WOKE UP AS THE faintest hint of light entered the morning sky, but it wasn't the light that caused us to rouse from our slumber. A large chorus of local birds provided the impetus for us to get up and investigate what was going on. We had been driving into the Black Forest in Germany while it was still dark the previous night, and since this was our first visit to this fabled region, I was anxious to experience it in the light of day. We stepped out onto the balcony of our room and could barely see anything, but the sound of all the birds was overwhelming. I have never heard so many birds in my life. It reinforced my high expectations for what the mythical Schwarzwald would be like. With my excitement building, Chris and I got ready for the day and stepped out to explore the forest. The air was cool and crisp, and there was frost on the ground from the night before. By this time, it was a bit lighter out, but not by much. As we looked across the gravel road in front of the hotel, we saw the forest in front of us like an ominous wall. It was dark, thick, and mysterious, just as the tales told by the Brothers Grimm indicated. I spied a path that entered into the woods and rapidly disappeared in the darkness of the trees. At this point my personality kicked in: I tend to look for the risks and boundaries of what is safe and adjust my plans accordingly. I began to consider that I didn't know where the path would lead or what we might come across. Did black bears still prowl these woods? Were there some cultural norms I might be breaking if we wandered into this area uninvited? I considered all the rules, conditions, and risk-assessments that percolated in my mind. Looking around, I saw a large grass field to our left. Instead of exploring the forest, I turned aside and we wandered into the field. Soon we heard the sound of a river and crossed the field to check it out. We found the river, lingered there for a few moments, and then wandered back to our hotel. As we entered the hotel, I cast a wary glance toward the woods, and then we packed our belongings and continued our trip. I immediately felt regret that I had not explored the forest, and that regret has always stayed with me.

A couple of months after my twenty-fifth birthday, I landed my dream job. I was hired on to work at what I considered to be the greatest company in the world, working for a large software developer in the Pacific Northwest. Less than two months into the job, I was shocked to wake up one morning to find a large lump protruding from the area between my ankle and Achilles tendon on my right leg. Emergency doctor visits, X-rays, CT scans, and MRIs led to multiple surgeries. I had a soft-tissue sarcoma—a type of cancer—growing from my right Achilles tendon. The doctors told me it was a medical impossibility to have that sort of cancer growing out from the Achilles tendon, but I guess I was the unfortunate exception to the medical rule. After surgeries and cancer treatments, I ended up losing the back half of my right leg, including most of the muscles and Achilles tendon itself. A donor tendon was sewn in its place to keep my foot from flopping around, but I would never again have the function in the leg that I once had. I could no longer jump, run, ski, stand on my toes, or push off from that foot. It was a permanent condition; it would never heal, grow back, and regain the strength necessary to do those things. In fact, the connection was so tenuous, I was told that even a slip on the stairs might cause it to snap. Due to the devastation caused by months of radiation, I was also told they would never be able to perform surgery on that area again. If something went wrong with the leg, such as the replacement tendon rupturing, they could not fix it. I was told to expect that the connections on the replacement tendon would only last for about ten years. Within that time, it was likely they would have to amputate the leg below the knee. I was glad to be alive and to have "beaten" the cancer, but it left its mark on me, and I was deeply depressed.

I thought about all the things I would not be able to do that had been a part of my life up to that point. Although not a father at this time in my life, I also realized that whenever I became a parent, I would not be able to do the fatherly things that I had pictured. I would not be the dad who ran down an errant Frisbee, played soccer with my kids, or jumped to catch a football that was thrown just a bit too high. I was very cautious with my activities as I didn't want to cause an injury to the leg that would lead to its amputation. Every activity that I approached, I always focused on the boundaries I could perceive and adjusted accordingly.

A few years later I was at a point where I was questioning what God's purpose in my life was. I wanted to be used by God, and I was crying out for Him to show me what to do. But I was also cautious and reluctant to takes chances. I was always performing risk-assessments and considering the logic of any path I would choose and where it might lead. One day I was driving home from work, and I was using my hour-plus commute as a time to speak with God. As I drove through the farmlands surrounding my community, He spoke to me. It wasn't an audible voice, but I heard Him in my heart. He showed me that morning back in the Schwarzwald where I looked at my mental boundaries and played it safe, missing the purpose I was there for in the first place. He made it clear to me that I had spent much of my life guessing where my boundaries were and trying to live within them, but He had other things for me if I would focus on Him instead of on my logic or limitations. For example, I had an application to a seminary sitting on my desk. I filled it out six months earlier but did not send it in because I was focused on my boundaries and couldn't make it fit within them. Things began to change that day.

I started focusing on God and less on my boundaries and limitations. Soon I was enrolled for an educational path that did not match my current career, and it led to something I never expected: a passion for theology and religion that ended with a PhD. I also began to reconsider the other limitations in my life, like the restrictions I placed upon myself due to the health of my right leg. I began to stretch what I was willing to do and began to enjoy more physical activities than I used to. That doesn't mean that I didn't have actual limitations. I still can't run, jump, etc. However, I enjoyed focusing on what I could do and found I could do more than I thought. I even ended up taking Krav Maga (an Israeli form of martial arts). Though I could not do everything most students could do, I took the risk and found myself doing something I never thought I would be able to do at all.

I eventually became a father, and my son is now nine years old. I write these words about an hour after playing a game of catch with my son. Sure enough, I could not jump to catch the balls he threw too high, and I could not run to catch balls thrown to the side like most dads can, but I don't think it mattered to Ephraim. And it really didn't matter to me either. My connection with my son was what was important, and I focused on that point of connection rather than on the boundaries in my life.

Discovering the Reality of Boundaries

Eating from the Tree of the Knowledge of Good and Evil brought about human comprehension of the concept of evil. Prior to eating from the Tree, Adam knew the goodness of God and of living a life that was perfectly centered on God. However, once he de-centered and became aware of evil—that he was capable of making poor choices that cause pain—he suddenly became aware of more than the center. He became aware of the boundaries he was not supposed to cross (and already had). After decentralizing and losing focus on the perfect will of God, he became cognizant of the myriad ways humans can sin. Adam went from knowing God and His goodness to becoming far more aware of the nature of boundaries. Boundaries are the multitude of forbidden things (thoughts, actions, intentions, etc.) that an individual should not do if one is truly focused on God. Before eating the forbidden fruit, Adam knew God. After eating the fruit, Adam's focus was turned away from God and toward the boundaries.

Watching the Boundaries

The bite of the serpent's lie had revealed its venom. Not only had Adam decentralized, but his attention became occupied by the overwhelming nature of his fallen state. There was only one narrow way to live a centered life; however, there were many ways to fail in the attempt. The knowledge of good and evil revealed to Adam the gravity of his new situation. You've probably heard the phrase, "ignorance is bliss." It was so very true. When God prohibited Adam from eating of the Tree, He was limiting Adam for his own sake. Gaining this knowledge can fundamentally change human existence, and not in a good way.[238] Once Adam knew of the boundaries, he could no longer focus just on the center. He was either too busy trying not to step over one of the boundaries, or he was trying to cover up the fact that he had already violated the boundaries, just like he did after he ate the fruit. "The man and his wife hid themselves from the presence of the LORD God among the trees of the garden" (Genesis 3:8b). He knew he had crossed a forbidden line. The imperfect finitude of human nature was contrasted against the infinite goodness of God, and the resulting difference was too overwhelming for them to face. The blissful ignorance that allowed perfect centering was gone, replaced by the boundary-aware timidity resulting from the first knowledge of evil. Just as humans are unable to reach from the earthly realm to the heavenly on their own, so the subsequent deeds of Adam could not recreate the connection he threw away. The finite cannot bridge to the infinite. Even our best efforts at perfection are now impacted by sin and evil, and we cannot live completely in line with how God wants us to.[239]

Observing the Boundaries Is Not Enough

With the divine connection severed, people started looking to the boundaries rather than to God. Lacking perfect centering, they paid attention to where they lived in relation to these boundaries. In other words, people tried to establish moral codes, rules, and social norms to draw attention to where the boundaries where. Eventually God gave Moses the Ten Commandments, and the tradition of the Law was established.

The Law tells people how to live. It codifies the boundaries. The Ten Commandments, along with all of the other regulations communicated in the Torah, contain a list of boundaries for modern living. For example, most of the Ten Commandments are a list of what *not* to do (in other words, established boundaries). Modern religions are very good at this. How many tens of thousands of Christian sermons have been preached on what people should not do? Islam is full of rules and interpretations, including Sharia law.[240] Judaism recognizes a list of things to do and a list of things not to do. One scholar noted that there are 365 prohibitions compared to 263 exhortations.[241]

However, the Law is not a formula for recreating the perpetual, sacred connection that Adam lost. It is not enough to do one's best to live within the lines. Many people feel that simply living a good life, or living a life that is generally within an individual's perception of the boundaries, is enough to earn a spot in heaven (which is the eternal renewal of sacred connection, space, and time). This view is a common problem even among many modern-day churches, which can be quite legalistic. Many who have spent time in churches have come away hearing many "do-nots," which have left them with the impression that if one does not cross the multitude of boundaries, one will be good enough to earn the favor of God. However, as Francis Schaeffer noted, "The fault of orthodoxy is that though it has a legal circle, it tends too often to act as though merely to be within the legal circle is enough."[242]

The truth is that a person cannot earn his or her way to heaven. To claim to be able to do enough good works to earn heaven is equivalent to saying that one is able to, by force of will and deed, establish the sacred connection from the earth to the heavens. This essentially ascribes God-like attributes to the finite, impure human. This is still the same lie of the serpent made manifest in thought and action: "you can be like God." The law does not teach us a way to re-establish the connection with God that was broken in the Fall. Instead, it shows our fallibility and demonstrates the need for the divine to reach down out of the heavens and establish a redemption connection on our behalf. It is a reminder to people that God alone is perfect and infinite, and we are imperfect and finite. "The law in this sense is not a ladder to heaven, but a closed circle, an impenetrable wall around our existence. It does not offer us a way out but tells rather the opposite: NO EXIT."[243] In becoming aware of the boundaries, we become aware of the hopelessness of attaining perfection and recreating the divine connection on our own.

Cannot Focus on Both God and the Boundaries

When teaching a series of classes on what would become this book, I rearranged the chairs in the room before discussing this specific topic. For this session, I arranged all the chairs in the room in a circle facing inward. While teaching from within the boundary of the circle with the students looking at me, it was easy for individuals to focus and to hear what was being taught. Partway through the class, I asked everyone to stand up, turn their chairs around, and sit facing the opposite direction from me. I then asked them to stare at either the wall or the floor. Staring at the wall or the floor was indicative of focusing on boundaries. Standing in the center of the circle with everyone's backs turned toward me, I continued to teach. However, it was difficult for the class to focus on me or on what was being taught. The experience was eye-opening for the participants in the class. The reality of their inability to focus on the center while watching the boundaries became a vivid example of the human condition.

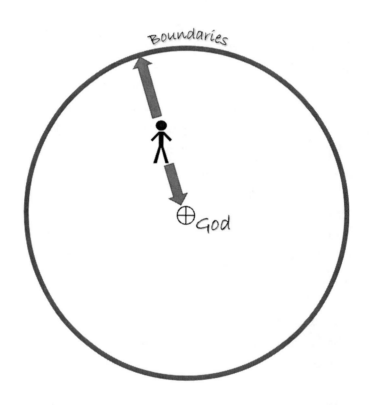

The overwhelming awareness of the boundaries is the first of many decentralizing distractions. When you focus on the boundaries, your focus cannot be on God. These boundaries are the delineation and quantification of evil. God is not evil. The boundaries and God *are not the same thing*, and you can have only one thing in focus at a time. A person's life spent carefully looking at the boundaries in an attempt not to cross forbidden lines is a life spent focused outward with his back turned toward God.

Read this very carefully: this is not to say that boundaries do not exist or to imply that boundaries are not important. God has specifically defined boundaries in the Bible for a reason. There are some things that are clearly called out as sin, and there some things that are even described as abominations. Nothing here changes that. Sin remains sin; abomination remains abomination.

However, the central focus of our lives is to be on God, not on the boundaries. When Jesus was asked which one of the commandments was the most important, he responded with a clear focus on God as the center. "You shall love the Lord your God with all your heart, and with all your soul, and with all your mind. This is the greatest and foremost commandment" (Matthew 22:37b-38). He took the focus of the people off of the boundaries and put it back on God.

Focusing on Other People in Relation to Boundaries

This leads to another aspect of decentralized focus. People often spend time looking at the lives of other individuals they know, and then they estimate where those individuals are in relation to their perception of a boundary. After all, every one of us has crossed the boundaries of righteousness. "For all have sinned and fall short of the glory of God" (Romans 3:23). Everyone sins. Everyone crosses a line. But our lives should be spent pointing to God, not pointing at laws and boundaries. Too many people focus on where other people stand in relation to the boundaries, and as such, their focus is still not on God. Christians are very good at spending time looking at where other people live in relation to the boundaries. However, the life of reconciliation is one that is focused on God, and effort is spent helping those who need God to make Him the center of their lives. We don't need to crucify people for their sins. We should seek redemption and healing for others, not inflict our own judgment. An example of this is shown when the Pharisees brought a woman to Jesus to be judged.

> The scribes and the Pharisees brought a woman caught in adultery, and having set her in the center of the court, they said to Him, "Teacher, this woman has been caught in adultery, in the very act. Now in the Law Moses commanded us to stone such women; what then do You say?" They were saying this, testing Him, so that they might have grounds for accusing Him. But Jesus stooped down and with His finger wrote on the ground. But when they persisted in asking Him, He straightened up, and said to them, "He who is without sin among you, let him be the first to throw a stone at her." Again he stooped down and wrote on the ground. When they heard it, they began to go out one by one, beginning with the older ones, and He was left alone, and the woman, where she was, in the center of the court. Straightening up, Jesus said to her, "Woman, where are they? Did no one condemn you?" She said, "No one, Lord." And Jesus said, "I do not condemn you, either. Go. From now on sin no more" (John 8:3-11).

This is a key passage. There is no denial that the woman had sinned. Jesus did not tell the woman "You have not sinned." Let us emphasize one more time that there is precisely zero declaration or implication of innocence anywhere in this passage. That the woman was a sinner, and that she was living outside the boundaries established by God, is unquestionable. She was caught in the middle of the act.

However, it was the accusers, the ones who pointed to her being outside the boundaries, who were sent away in shame. The motivation of the accusers is made clear with a careful reading of the passage. Their request of Jesus was not whether or not the lady could be reconciled to God; their request was to kill her, which would send her straight to eternal judgment. They also wanted to test Jesus so that they could attack him. In no way did these Pharisees focus on God. They perceived Jesus as a mere human, and their testing of him was an effort to make him cross a boundary and prove himself imperfect. Instead, Jesus sent away those who were focused on people and boundaries, and then he redirected the sinful woman to a reconciled life focused on God. He sought to draw the woman, who was living on the other side of the boundary, into a God-focused life. His refusal to condemn her was not erasure of the boundary. Rather, Jesus stood beside her, lifted her eyes up off of the boundary that pronounced her shame and brokenness, and placed her focus on the loving grace and forgiveness of God. "The law of love will not draw a line because lines divide. The law of love transgresses all lines and stands 'at-one' with the other."[244]

The best way to not cross a boundary is to focus on God. If you're focusing on God as you move through life, you will naturally move closer to God and further away from the boundaries. With other people, we want to encourage them to join us as friends in our journey focused on God, and in a similar fashion, should they choose to do so, they will also naturally walk closer to God and away from the boundaries.

Off-Center Lives That Intersect with God-Centered Actions

Life is full of people who do some amazingly kind and loving things for others. They come from all walks of life, and they represent every faith group imaginable. It is not only Christians who do good things. Many of these people are not focused on God as the center of their lives, yet they still feel fulfilled and valuable. Many of them would also say that they feel good spiritually about how they are living. I understand how people can feel good about their existential situation in the cosmos when they do these things. For example, look at someone who is a good parent and raises children well. This is good and fulfilling. Another example might be someone who does valuable charity work. Perhaps another example would be someone who fights crime. A comprehensive list of examples would go on for a very long time. These are all very good things that will provide someone with a sense of fulfillment. It feels good and spiritually right because these good works are works which ultimately point to God as the center.

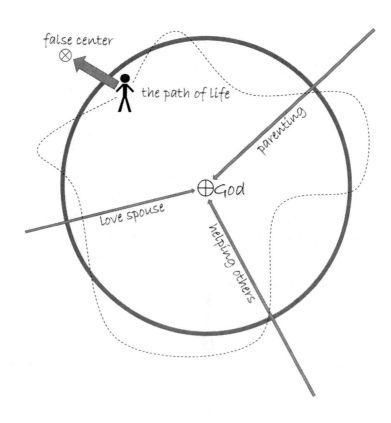

At any given point in time, the line of an individual's life may cross with the line of an action that is rooted in the goodness and truth of the absolute, divine center. I picture these good actions as emanating out and pointing to God in the center. The path of a person's life crosses one of these lines when they perform one of these good tasks or roles. Think of Joe who is a great father. The path of his life intersects with the line of being a great parent. The line of being a great parent is something that comes from God and points to Him. Intersecting with a line that comes from and points to God can and does happen to most people, even if their focus is not on the God of the Bible. This can even happen for someone who is completely outside the boundaries. The intersection of a life with a line that points to God will produce a hint and a confirmation of what is found in a life that is centered on God, part of which is true fulfillment. Hence, a life path that intersects one of these God-facing lines should produce positive reinforcement. However, simply intersecting a line is not the same thing as truly being centered on God. We must be careful not to allow a temporary sense of fulfillment to replace or distract the need for a life that unswervingly points to and is centered on God.

Ultimately, living a life that is centered on God (as best as one can) is very difficult. Individuals are too aware of the boundaries, too distracted by and too focused on things that are not the true center. Even for those who know the truth on an intellectual level, it can be difficult to live a centered life consistently. Intellectual assent to the truth of focusing on God is one thing; actually living a God-focused life is another. And our drive toward individual freedom often trips us up.

᭥ CHAPTER 17: ᭥

Freedom—The Illusion and the Lie

NESTLED QUIETLY ON A HILL in the northwest part of Bavaria, Rothenburg ob der Tauber is the archetype of a medieval cobblestoned village. A stone wall surrounds the old town, while fragrant restaurants and beautiful stores beckon to people wandering peacefully along its streets. It is picturesque and peaceful, and as a result, tourists have been coming to Rothenburg for many years. However, during the Second World War, Allied forces bombed the town, leaving some parts of it heavily damaged. As soon as the war ended, people from all over the world (including many from the Allied countries) began to contribute thousands of dollars in an effort to restore the beauty and charm of this favored village. Today, if you climb the stairs up to the top of the wall, you can walk its entire length, and all along the reconstructed wall, you can see bricks engraved with the names of significant donors. The reconstruction of Rothenburg was a marvelous success, and if no one told you, you might never know about the rebuilding efforts.

There are two specific signs in one particular location of the town that share the story of the city. One sign is in English and the other in German. While vacationing there, a friend who was visiting the city for the first time (I had been there a few times before) read the English sign. It took a mostly neutral, fact-based view on the damage done by the Allies and the cooperative rebuilding effort after the war. The German sign stood next to it, and the writing on that one was a bit longer than the writing on the English sign. After noting the difference in length, my friend made a comment that the German sign must contain a lot of information that was not on the English sign. From his personal point of cultural reference (fluency in English but no experience with German), it seemed logical to conclude that the longer German sign said more than the English sign. From there it was easy to guess (with no malice intended) that the sign would favor a local German perspective on the bombing, one less complimentary about the Allied role in rebuilding due to the possibly unnecessary damage the Allies caused during the war. My cultural background was helpful in this situation. I joked that I speak bad English and worse German, and I explained that the average word length in German is longer than in English. As an example, given the many years I spent in the software industry (including at that time), I pointed out that when localizing programs from English to other languages, software companies often translate to German first. Since the German words are typically much longer, this allows them to see if the text in their software exceeds the programmed display boundaries (if words get cut off, if they overlap, and so on). With regard to the German and English signs, there was no significant disparity in their content despite the difference in length.

I can understand why my friend assumed the German sign had more content than the English sign. He applied his English point of reference to judge a German language issue, and so his analysis or guess—even with the best of intentions—ended up being incorrect. Sometimes we perceive something as true that simply isn't. Sometimes it's unintentional, sometimes it's the consequence of deceit, and sometimes it's self-deceit. My friend is very open-minded and was willing to hear that his perception might have been off. Unfortunately for many of us, we're not so willing to accept we might be wrong. Perhaps nowhere in history was this more impactful than in the Garden.

Freedom

We often think of true freedom as having the ability to do anything we want without anyone or anything inhibiting our own self-determination in any way. One dictionary's primary definition of freedom is, "the condition of being free from restraints."[245] This thought is common. It is also something that simply does not, and will not ever, exist.

The freedom of a finite being is always limited by the context in which the finite being exists. In other words, the nature of finite human existence means there are natural conditions and restraints placed upon every individual. For a human, there is no such thing as pure freedom in the traditional sense of the word. Many people would agree with this to a limited extent since a human is obviously not all-powerful and cannot do anything he or she wishes to do. For example, a human cannot extinguish the sun. However, human freedom is actually far more limited than this extreme example. Human freedom is limited by the existential condition of humanity.

Before proceeding further, the context for this position must be firmly established. This is not an attempt to analyze the entirety of the subject of freedom in every sense of the word. Also, this is not an attempt to deal with certain concepts of freedom that philosophers and theologians apply in their works, such as libertarian versus compatibilist freedom. This is *not* an attempt to take any side in the debate between Calvinism, Arminianism, Molinism, or any other soteriological "-ism." Rather, it analyzes the reality of reconciling the common human concept of freedom (no restraints, complete self-determinism) with the concept of God as the absolute center.

Contextual Freedom

We're going to start with what might be an intimidating sentence: In order to be truly self-determining for more than an instant, an individual's choice must actualize potential freedom in a way that does not decrease contextual freedom, and it must be sustainable within that context. Let's break this down in a way that is easy to understand.

There are many choices a person can make. Simply having the ability to make a choice does not mean that the choice will lead to the experience of freedom. Since humans are finite, we are contextually limited by our finitude. Any choice for true freedom will be a choice that *wholly lines up within God's designed context for human existence*. It will also be a choice that will be actualized for more than just the instant when the choice is made—the choice must lead to continued freedom over time.

One example of this is of a young man who purchases a brand-new convertible with low clearance. While driving around in his shiny new car, he can make the momentary choice to drive off of the paved roads and on to rough terrain. This is indeed an instantaneous choice he is able to make. However, if he does that, his car will be severely damaged and cease functioning properly. This would happen because he has not obeyed the existential context for which the engineers specifically designed the car: smooth, paved roads. He must follow their specific, designed driving context in order to sustain the driving freedom the vehicle provides. That context was established by the designer's superior knowledge of what style of driving would provide the maximum, sustainable, safe experience. The choice to use the car outside of the designer's context actually limits the freedom of the driver by destroying the function of the car or by hurting himself.

He could spend his entire transportation budget on this car and then promptly make the choice to treat it as if it is a boat. He can drive down to the pier and race off the end, landing in the sea. If he did this, people would not praise him for actualizing freedom via self-determination. They would call him an idiot.

Some choices will lead to less freedom.[246] Some instantaneous choices violate existential context and limit or destroy long-term contextual freedom, just like the convertible that is now part of a coral reef.

True Freedom Is Sustainable

All humans exist in a given context, just like the young man's convertible has a context. As previously demonstrated, God is the center for humanity. He is the source of life, and He defines absolute truth. An individual might think of freedom as the ability to go as far away from something as he or she desires. However, *true freedom is found in moving closer to the center*, not in the distance one can travel away from the center. For the Christian, there is no pure freedom. There is only the contextual freedom that comes from our creation. The context for our existence is given to us by God. He sets boundaries on our freedom, just as He did with all creation. This was displayed as far back as the cosmogony.

> When God creates, God liberates. The creation song of Genesis 1 depicts a God who frees earth from chaos and from the destructive beast. God sets the cosmos free. Yet God also establishes limits for the freed cosmos by setting boundaries between the earth and the heavens, the earth and the seas, day and night. So already in God's act of creation, freedom is defined and confined by boundaries.[247]

The Lie of Self-Determination

Part of the serpent's lie is that he implied the possibility of true self-determination. The serpent told Eve that she could make her own choices, that she would not suffer the consequences that were promised, that she would have knowledge to continue to make choices, and that she would be like God. However, Adam and Eve were not truly free to self-determine their lives. At the Fall, the truth of the limits and the conditions of humanity's existential state came into full effect. For them, suddenly their lives had far less freedom than before. The serpent promised freedom in complete self-determination, but God knew that freedom only truly existed within the context and limitations that He had established. Bonhoeffer described the competing views of freedom as, "God's truth connected with the prohibition, the serpent's truth connected with the promise, God's truth pointing to my limit, the serpent's truth pointing to my limitlessness."[248] The serpent lied and achieved the destruction he desired when Adam chose to try to live outside humanity's existential context.

True freedom comes only from God. The human experience of ultimate freedom is found in living a life that points to the center. The limit of true freedom is not found by looking to see how large the boundaries are or how far you can travel beyond them. Looking at boundaries takes the focus off of the source of freedom (God). True freedom only exists along that thin, perfect path that leads from an individual's life directly to God. It is the path where human effort will achieve the greatest net result for the expenditure of energy. Any deviation from the path that points directly to God is not an exercise of freedom, *it is a momentary choice to voluntarily diminish one's own freedom.*

A Choice to Diminish Freedom

Since humans are created in a context, acting within that context is the path of freedom. As seen in the story of the Garden, it is also the only way for humans to truly live. The choice Adam made in the Garden was a choice to attempt to live outside of the line of context that points directly to God. By using a different center as his chosen context, he ignored the true context that limited his existential state. At that very moment, Adam fell into bondage. He had to work the earth to eat; he was mortal and separated from the source of life; he was going to die. The life that was easy and fulfilling was lost to him, and it was replaced by a life of hard work that would yield lesser results. No sane person would quantify Adam's choice as a choice for freedom. Our world is now fallen and we live under the curse. This means our freedom is already very limited to start with. Paul described this to the believers in Rome:

> I am of flesh, sold into bondage to sin. For what I am doing, I do not understand; for I am not practicing what I would like to do, but I am doing the very thing I hate. . . . So now, no longer am I the one doing it, but sin which dwells in me. For I know that nothing good dwells in me, that is, in my flesh; for the willing is present in me, but the doing of the good is not. For the good that I want, I do not do, but I practice the very evil that I do not want (Romans 7:14b-15, 17-19).

A practical example of this is drug addiction. People can make the choice to use dangerous, addictive narcotics. However, the use of those narcotics will not lead to freedom but to bondage. As addiction sets in, the drug starts to become a new center for addicts, and it can easily start to affect all decision-making and life choices. Some addicts lose jobs, families, and even their lives. The destruction of freedom will often spread to friends and family as well. Like the serpent's lie, the illusory freedom they were promised led them into a bondage from which they cannot escape.

The choice to decentralize from the perfect source of life and freedom is the choice to enter into a state of diminished freedom. The positive, powerful attributes of human existence are turned away from the goodness of God and now work to drag an individual further away from the narrow path of authentic freedom. The freedom from that downward spiral is found only in God.

Freedom from Bondage

Humans are always bound by context set by God. However, once Adam sinned, the context for human existence now included the power and bondage of sin. As soon as Adam decentralized off of God and on to someone or something else, he could not recapture that perfect centering he had in the beginning. Like a spinning top that has lost its perfect point of balance and begins to wobble in wider and wider circles as its momentum moves away from the center, the perfect center for human existence cannot be regained by human effort alone. Once it is really out of balance and loses its energy, the top will topple. In the same way, humans cannot regain perfect centering on their own. This is where Christ enters into the picture. Jesus, as God incarnate, is the center for modern humanity. The sacrifice of Christ on the Cross broke the power of sin over humans. The message of the Cross is "that our old self was crucified with Him, in order that our body of sin might be done away with, so that we would no longer be slaves to sin; for he who has died is freed from sin" (Romans 6:6-7). This is the external power necessary to free someone from self-imposed, downward-spiraling bondage. The sacrifice of Christ is what corrects the imbalance and decentralization in humanity, if we allow it to by accepting his work on our behalf. This is what starts the top spinning with its perfect centering restored. Paul described this new freedom from bondage as being "dead to sin, but alive to God in Christ Jesus" (Romans 6:14). However, Paul did not indicate that freedom from sin leads to complete, context-free self-determination. Rather, it resets the context for existence away from the sin-saturated bondage induced by the Fall to the freedom of God.

> Having been freed from sin, you became slaves of righteousness . . . For just as you presented your members as slaves to impurity and to lawlessness, resulting in further lawlessness, so now present your members as slaves to righteousness, resulting in sanctification (Romans 6:18-19).

Paul says that the Christian has ceased to be in bondage to sin, but is now in bondage to the center (Jesus). Paul even introduces himself as "Paul, a bond-servant [slave] of Christ-Jesus" (Romans 1:1a). However, being a slave to Christ is really just another way of saying "being free to truly live." The sacrifice of Christ is what enables us to live a life pointing to God, which could not be done under the bondage of sin and the weight of the curse.[249] For us there is no greater freedom than the freedom to live fully for God. This is the most important freedom there is.[250]

Christ-Centered Freedom Is Unique for Each Individual

God knows best how each individual will experience maximum, sustainable, contextual freedom. God created the cosmos, and He knows exactly how we function best. Some limits He set on our existence are inviolable. For example, an individual cannot exist in all places at all times. That is part of our finite, profane nature. Other limits, such as the prohibition not to eat from the Tree of the Knowledge of Good and Evil, can be violated. But, as was demonstrated in the story of the Garden, Adam's momentary choice to self-determine to live a life that was not centered on God led to bondage. The limits He places on us are the signposts that lead the way to our enjoyment of a life full of freedom. You can either decide to live a life of contextual freedom, or you choose to struggle against the context. You either choose to rely on yourself or you choose to center and rely on Christ.

Living the true freedom found in a Christ-centered existence is the path to living a fulfilled life. However, it is not a path of diminished individuality and personality. God created and knows everyone individually. The path of freedom that leads to the center, the path of the Christian to be "Christ-like," will look different for each person.

A theoretical center can be approached from an infinite number of points, and each line that approaches the center occupies a different space and is unique from the nearby lines that also point to the center. The Christian life is the same. There isn't one specific occupation that a follower of Christ must pursue. There isn't one specific set of skills that must be developed, or one type of humor, or one set of hobbies. The proper Christian community isn't a collection of people who are all the same. Rather, it is a wonderful group of different individuals with different personalities, skills, enthusiasms, backgrounds, and passions. They are bound together in their freedom to individually pursue the path that leads to Christ at the center.

Examining Your Freedom

Now is a good time to take a moment to consider the state of freedom in your life. Are you struggling against the context of your existence? Have you found yourself in bondage as the result of choices you thought were self-determining? Consider if this is a good time to take a break and ask God for help. I encourage you to talk to Him verbally if possible and appropriate. Let Him know that you realize that true freedom is found only when centered on Him, and you want to re-center on Him. If you've never surrendered ownership of your life to Jesus in the first place, then now is a good time to make that part of your prayer as well. It's time to start living the fullness of freedom by centering on Jesus.

CHAPTER 18

Centered, Connected Living

IT'S MAY 7, 2017, AND as I sit outside on a sunny spring day, I have been considering what words I should use to introduce this chapter. All the content of the book is now written with the exception of figuring out what story to share to introduce this section's concepts. I've been pacing around in the sunlight deep in thought and prayer, but I've been struggling to find the right words—until something happened this afternoon.

Some family history will be relevant here. My mother was given up for adoption at birth, and she became part of a great, loving family. They were the only family she knew in her life, and her adoptive parents were her authentic parents and my authentic grandparents. She could not have loved them more. But she had questions about who her birth parents were and she was curious about their circumstances.

About a year ago the adoptee services notified my mom that her birth mother had passed, and this meant my mom was able to at least have her name, if not much more. Based on what little data we had about the circumstances surrounding her birth, we suspected that no one in the family knew my mother existed. Through some great sleuthing, my wife was able to locate an in-law of the birth family and reached out to make contact. We were all very nervous. The family of her birth mother was very surprised to find out my mom existed. Sure enough, no one knew. DNA testing confirmed their relationship, and soon we were welcomed into an amazing family. My mother was surprised to find out she had three sisters, one of whom had passed but two of whom were still alive. Connecting with her birth-mother's family has been an amazing experience for her, and it has brought healing to both her and to her birth family. The more we connect, the more we realize how great these connections are that we didn't know we needed in our lives.

Meeting this family in no way replaces my mom's adopted parents, who have long since passed away, but it's hard to describe how meaningful these new connections have been to her (and to me as well). People like Jan, Mary, and Kenton, among many great new family members, stand out as being incredible people, and our lives are richer for being around them. However, no one knew who the birth father was, and no one was listed on any of the documentation, including on the birth certificate. That part of her life would remain a dead end.

As I was struggling today to find a story for the start of this chapter—the final words I need to write for this book—my wife came out onto the back patio with a special look on her face while talking on the cell phone. My wife's investigative skills, coupled with an ever-increasing DNA database, led to her finding my mother's birth father. She had reached out to people who were DNA relatives on the birth-father's side and was able to narrow things down until the birth-father's name was revealed. In the first few hours after this discovery, these newly discovered family members are proving receptive and welcoming. My mother has already been on the phone with one of her newly found first cousins, and they are both surprised and excited to welcome her to meet this supposedly large side of the family.

So when Chris walked out onto the patio earlier today and handed me the phone, I heard my mom's voice on the other end. She was sobbing tears of both joy and amazement; she was utterly overwhelmed. She emphasized again how much she loved her adoptive parents and that no one would ever replace them, but she was amazed at how important finding these new points of connection were to her. She always had an intellectual desire to know about her birth, but she never expected that she would ever emotionally connect with the family she never knew and never expected to find. She was filled with joy as she described her surprise at how meaningful it was to connect with these people. My mom's always been great at connecting with people. But now more than ever, and in a deeper way than she ever expected, she is expanding her understanding of what it means to live a connected life. Living a life connected with others, and with God above all, is an essential part of our existence.

Christ-Centered Living

As we approach the end of this book, let's quickly remind ourselves of what we have covered. The Bible is full of ancient myths, symbols, and rituals. The ancient myths, symbols, and rituals found in scripture were not unique to the early people of the Bible. These same (or similar) practices were found all over the ancient world. When time is taken to carefully study the underlying form of all of the practices, the concept of *living centrism* emerges.

The ancient people believed that the ancient manifestations of the sacred were real, and that they were sources of absolute, existential truth. As external sources of absolute truth, the ancients valued these manifestations as more than just mere intellectual truth—they were intrinsic reference points for life. A coherent system of religious practices consisting of the myths, symbols, and rituals developed.

All of these religious practices pointed to a center. The sacred was viewed as being central to all existence. The center provided orientation and value for living, and the center was where humanity could commune with the divine. For a religious person, particularly a Christian, living life oriented on the divine is the true manifestation of a religious symbol.[251]

The Bible gives many examples of these ancient practices. Some are used as examples of evil and idolatry, but other examples appear to be condoned. Many are explicitly requested by God. All of the myths, symbols, and rituals point to the absolute, central role of God in human living. Christ, as God incarnate, is the ultimate center. Jesus is the ultimate hierophany. As such, he is the living, personal axis mundi—the exclusive way for humans to connect with the true divine.

It was the centrality of God in life that Adam had in the Garden. It was his decentralization off of God that led to the Fall. Gaining knowledge of good and evil led to the overwhelming awareness of boundaries. While boundaries really do exist—there are such things as "right and wrong"—the knowledge of the boundaries has proven to be a tremendous distraction when trying to live a centered life. Even the most well-meaning of believers can often centralize their lives on staying within the boundaries as opposed to explicitly living for the center.

True, sustainable freedom also comes from God, who is the center. A choice to self-determine and to live a life that does not line up directly with the center is actually a voluntary choice to diminish one's own freedom. After the Fall, humankind fell into the bondage of sin. Christ, who is God incarnate and the center, died in order to break the bondage of sin and make it possible for humanity to realign with God as the center. This allowed humankind to reacquire the true freedom that Adam lost. God does not provide rules and limits in order to reign in individuality and expression; rather, God does it to help people avoid making poor choices that would end up limiting their contextual freedom.

Since the ancient people lived as though the divine was the absolute center and guide for their lives, since the concept of centrism is in the Bible (and indeed appears to have originated in the Garden of Eden), and since the role of Christ as the redeeming center for the world is made clear in scripture, it follows that all Christians of all times should take the ancient concept of *living centrism* and apply it to their lives. For the modern Christian, that means living a life with Christ as the absolute center. This is more than the mere, intellectual assent to Christ as the ideological center; it is the divine mandate to live a life oriented on and pointing to God at all times. I call this theology of Christian living, "Christocentrism."

What Christ-Centered Living IS NOT

When approaching the definition of a topic, I believe it is important to state what something *is not* as well as state what that something actually is. We're going to cover this briefly here.

Christ-centered living is not an alternative to the whole truth of the Bible. You cannot just throw away parts of the Bible in your extreme emphasis on Christ. The whole of the Bible points to him in some fashion, and it is all valid for the believer.

Christ-centered living is not accepting of all religious beliefs. Jesus Christ himself said, "I am the way, and the truth, and the life; no one comes to the Father *but through Me*" (John 14:6, emphasis added). Buddha, Allah, Krishna, or good works will not get you close to the true God. While we have looked at other religious myths, symbols, and rituals, we did this to inform our context for understanding religious patterns, not because they point to the God of the Bible. They are not the center; Jesus is.

Christ-centered living is not a political party. Many God-centered Christians belong to different political parties (or none at all), and many hold to differing views on specific issues. While godly views may impact one's political views, Christ-centered living is about *Christ, not politics.*

Christ-centered living is neither a validation nor a condemnation of one particular generational style compared to another. Baby boomers, Gen Xers, millennials, and others are all part of God's created and loved family. Nothing in this book should be taken as supporting one generational personality over another.

Having made some brief statements about what Christ-centered living is not (I'm sure there are more than what I listed here), let's move on to the good stuff. We'll do this by looking at examples of what Christocentrism looks like in life. This is not an exhaustive list. Consider this a starting point for discussion and something to jump-start your thought process about how to apply Christocentrism in your personal life.

Christocentrism: Centered Theology

Since the Bible is a book of God-inspired truth about (among other things of existential value) God and Jesus, theology is the first area where Christocentrism should be applied. Obviously Christian theology has a focus on the person and work of Christ in particular. Not much needs to be mentioned here, except for a reminder to keep it focused on Christ as revealed by the inspired, inerrant word of God. Theology should never be centered on modern societal directions or movements. There is no need to keep theology current for society; there is only a need to keep theology true because God is absolute truth. In that regard, it is important to center theology on the absolute center of truth and meaning rather than allowing it to become a malleable tool of politics, society, or public opinion. What is taught in churches, in Christian schools, and in seminaries must reflect the absolute, divine, unchanging truth. It must not mold itself to the current trends of popular thought, which are nothing more than any given day's most popular form of decentralization.

Centered theology must refuse to be an instrument manipulated to improper ends by church leadership or congregational majority; it must refuse simply to reflect what people believe at a given point in time. Instead, it should be so overwhelmed by the joy of the gospel that it fearlessly examines the faith and practice of the church in light of the gospel and courageously accepts its function of being a thorn in the flesh of the church.[252]

This is the role of centered theology: to remind everyone that Christ is the absolute, true, unchanging center. He is the ultimate hierophany and the supreme axis mundi. Centered theology must be based on the immutable revelation of the Bible and never on popular opinion.

Christocentrism: Centered Fellowship

A life spent moving toward God is a life that simultaneously draws other people toward God. However, Christians often do not appear to get along even with one another. The (apparently healing) division in northern Ireland, partially cast as a conflict between Catholics and Protestants, is one recent, extreme example of Christians who are centered on other people or politics and not God. There are already so many divisions in the world, and the people of Christ do need to be tearing each other apart.[253] Even within denominations, people can be brutal to their fellow Christians. Petty arguments and minor disagreements can often lead to wounded relationships within a church. No church is immune.

At times when hurting people need the support of fellow Christians the most—in the throes of addiction or in the midst of divorce—the publicly obvious sins and failures often lead to ostracizing a struggling individual (although sometimes people also choose to ostracize themselves). This is not the Christ-centered fellowship of the Bible. If the church cannot care for and love its own, then how can it claim to have a message of hope and joy for the rest of the world?

Centered fellowship is the joy that was experienced by the first Christians. In fact, they did more than provide emotional support, they provided physical and financial support (see Acts 4:32-35). They made personal sacrifices to take care of the distressed among them rather than leaving them to wallow in misery and suffering. The truly Christ-centered church of modern times needs to be a church that acknowledges the truth of Christ-centered theology and then puts that theology to practice in its own personal relationships and church fellowship. Christ-centered fellowship does not divide; it draws others closer to Christ. In doing so, it heals. The church should be comprised of people centered on Christ and in fellowship with each other. This is the meaning of centered fellowship. This is the type of fellowship a Christocentric church should model for its congregants.

Christocentrism: Centered Relationships

When asked what the most important commandment was, Jesus responded with, "You shall love the Lord your God with all your heart, and with all your soul, and with all your mind" (Matthew 22:37b). However, he also went on to say, "You shall love your neighbor as yourself. On these two commandments depend the whole Law and the prophets" (Matthew 22:39b-40). The importance of the second commandment should not be ignored. From Christ himself—from the absolute center—the command is given to all believers to love others the same as they love themselves. Quite often, however, the Christian's relationship with non-believers is not one of equal love. Christ's command is not for mere intellectual acquiescence to the concept of loving another as an individual loves oneself, but rather it is a command for a life that is actually lived (deliberate action) with outward, genuine love toward our neighbors. It is not an intellectual position; it is a lifestyle.

This does not refer to a feeling of love, but to love made manifest in action. Our feelings will then fall in line with our actions.[254]

Christians must practice Christ-centered acts of reconciliation with regard to their relationships with those who do not profess to share their beliefs. A person's position in relation to being beyond the boundaries is not the important part. God earnestly desires the love of and salvation of all people. The Christian approach should mimic God's approach. This may not seem to be an outrageous or extraordinary statement; however, in terms of real application and authentic action, it may be foreign to some Christians.

The command to love one's neighbor is not a command to believe that everything that a neighbor does is acceptable in the sight of God. One of the fallacies promoted by modern society is that tolerance does not view anything as wrong. That is not tolerance at all; that is syncretism. Tolerance actually implies disagreement or difference. It does not imply uniformity. However much a Christian might disagree with a neighbor on a particular issue, the Christian is still commanded by Christ to love that person. The relationship with one's neighbor is a vital part of living a Christ-centered life. A person who is living a Christ-centered life makes the outward-facing, healing love of God a conscious, integral part of their relationships with all people. This is centered living.

Christocentrism: Centered Service

The Christ-centered life manifests its Christ-centeredness in meeting the needs of the world around it. James, the brother of Jesus, wrote, "Pure and undefiled religion is this: to visit orphans and widows in their distress, and to keep oneself unstained by the world" (James 1:27). According to James, it appears that if an individual truly has Christ as the center of his or her life, then that individual's lifestyle will reflect it with caring action for others. However, it is common for the outside world to think that the main things Christians do is gather in a church on Sunday mornings.[255] That is quite an indictment of just how Christ-centered Christians are perceived to be by the rest of the world.

To be fair, many people are probably not aware of the impact that the church has had in meeting the needs of the world. The church has done more for people in need than any government ever has. Regardless of perception versus reality, Christians ought to be deliberate about reaching out to take care of the needs of those around them.

During the famous Sermon on the Mount, Jesus preached what is known as the beatitudes (Matthew 5:3-12). The beatitudes are a beautiful illustration of Christ-centeredness. However, the beatitudes are more than a mere pronouncement of "blessed are . . ." They are a distinct call to action for those who would claim to follow (center their lives on) Christ. They are a call for centered service.

For instance, Christ calls those who serve the needy "blessed." In the first days of the church, the early believers made deliberate efforts to care for those in need. Acts 6:1-6 tells of the apostles specifically appointing people to take care of ensuring that all their needy are taken care of. Acts 11:28-30 tells of how supplies were gathered in one region to be sent to another region to assist with an upcoming famine. These early examples of Christ-centered service are what helped establish the church in a hostile environment. The early church exemplified centered service.

> The solidarity of Christians was unequaled; the community took care of widows, orphans, and the aged and ransomed those captured by pirates. During epidemics and sieges, only Christians tended the wounded and buried the dead. For all the rootless multitudes of the Empire, for the many who suffered from loneliness, for the victims of cultural and social alienation, the Church was the only hope of obtaining an identity, of finding, or recovering, a meaning for life. Since there were no barriers, either social, racial, or intellectual, anyone could become a member of this optimistic and paradoxical society in which a powerful citizen, the emperor's chamberlain, bowed before a

bishop who had been his slave. In all probability, neither before nor afterward has any historical society experienced the equivalent of this equality, of the charity and brotherly love that were the life of the Christian communities of the first four centuries.[256]

This sort of sacrificial service is exactly what Christ meant when he said to "love your neighbor as yourself." In following Christ's command to love others, one also loves Christ. If there is any doubt about this, it should be put to rest by the words of Christ himself.

But when the Son of Man comes in His glory, and all the angels with Him, then He will sit on His glorious throne. All the nations will be gathered before Him; and He will separate them from one another, as the shepherd separates the sheep from the goats; and He will put the sheep on His right, and the goats on the left. Then the King will say to those on His right, "Come, you who are blessed of My Father, inherit the kingdom prepared for you from the foundation of the world. For I was hungry, and you gave Me something to eat; I was thirsty, and you gave Me something to drink; I was a stranger, and you invited Me in; naked, and you clothed Me; I was sick, and you visited Me; I was in prison, and you came to Me." Then the righteous will answer Him, "Lord, when did we see You hungry, and feed You, or thirsty, and give You something to drink? And when did we see You a stranger, and invite You in, or naked, and clothe You? When did we see You sick, or in prison, and come to You?" The King will answer and say to them, "Truly I say to you, to the extent that you did it to one of these brothers of Mine, even the least of them, you did it to Me." Then He will also say to those on His left, "Depart from Me, accursed ones, into the eternal fire which has been prepared for the devil and his angels; for I was hungry, and you gave Me nothing to eat; I was thirsty, and you gave Me nothing to drink; I was a stranger, and you did not invite Me in; naked, and you did not clothe Me; sick, and in prison, and you did not visit Me." Then they themselves also will answer, "Lord, when did we see You hungry, or thirsty, or a stranger, or naked, or sick, or in prison, and did not take care of You?" Then He will answer them, "Truly I say to you, to the extent that you did not do it to one of the least of these, you did not do it to Me" (Matthew 25:31-45).

These words are a powerful affirmation of centered service; likewise, they serve as an equally powerful condemnation of the absence of centered service. That is not to say that engaging in centered service means that an individual must go so far as to abandon his or her current vocation and find a new one that serves the needy. Rather, it says that if we are truly centered on Christ, then God's love will manifest through the actions of our lives in ways that impact those in need. This is the sacred duty of the individual Christian as well as the church as a whole.

Christocentrism

As we bring this topic to a close, may we all be challenged to center our lives on Jesus. All of the passages in the Bible, including the mysterious myths, symbols, and rituals, point to Christ as the center. Thorwald Lorenzen says it well:

> All our thinking and doing, our talk of values, and our engagement for justice, need to have a ground, a basis, a foundation, something that was there before and that outlasts the ambiguity and uncertainty of the moment, something stronger than our fears and inability to understand, something that transcends our experience and commitments. For Christians that something is someone, *Jesus Christ*.[257]

Epilogue

A MAN WALKS DOWN THE street and takes in the sights. Although he's lived here a long time, the wonders of the city never cease to amaze him. They didn't have cities like this when he was young. "Actually," he thinks to himself, "there's never been a city like this in all of history. This is truly one of a kind."

He spies a nearby bridge and strolls leisurely across it, stopping to spend some time watching the clear, sparkling water pass underneath, smiling to himself as he recalls the rivers from his past. Turning upstream, he sees the water cascading downhill after passing underneath the roots of a huge tree that span the river. Drawn by the scent of ripe fruit, he walks off the bridge and follows a path up the hillside and along the river. Moving past the tree, he casually plucks one of the pieces of fruit and continues to follow the river up to its source in the center of town. As he approaches the top of hill at the city center, he turns around to enjoy a view of the city while savoring a bite of fresh fig.

A voice interrupts his reverie, "Shalom, L'Shana Tovah." The man keeps admiring the view of the city, not turning around to look at the speaker. He doesn't need to look; he knows the voice of his old friend.

"Shalom, viShana Tovah," he replies in the predominant language of the city. It's not quite the same language he spoke with his friend in his younger days. It's changed over time, but it's similar. He spends a moment gazing at all the people moving about on the streets below, making a small gesture in their general direction. "There are so many," he says, pausing as he processes his thoughts. He continues quietly, his voice cracking with emotion, "And I caused so much trouble." He feels his friend's hand squeeze his shoulder in a reassuring gesture. "What the other meant for evil . . . " the friend said in a kind voice. There was no need to finish the thought.

"Indeed," the man answered, "Thank you for taking care of it."

"I'd do it again," came the earnest reply.

"I know you would." A noise from the center of town drew the man's attention and provided an opportunity to change topics. "I'm looking forward to the festival tonight," he announced. "Which vintner is providing the wine?"

"Dave," answered his friend.

"*The* Dave?" asked the man excitedly, seeking confirmation.

"Yes, that Dave. I'm really looking forward to it," said the friend with genuine enthusiasm.

"Then we better get going so we don't miss any of it," the man said. He turned and looked pointedly at his old friend from ages past. "It's almost as if Dave has been given a special gift."

"Yes, it's as if he has," said the friend with a knowing smile. "Let's get going then." He drapes his arm around the man's shoulder, his oldest friend, and together they walk to the top of the hill in the center of the city, connected with one another, as they were always meant to be.

Ὁ κύριός μου καὶ ὁ θεός μου

About the Author

ERIC ODELL-HEIN IS THE PRESIDENT of Columbia Evangelical Seminary, a seminary where the ministry focus is meeting the educational needs of those who do not have easy access to a local seminary education. He earned a bachelor of theology, a master of religious studies in world religions, a master of divinity in practical theology, and a PhD in theology with a study emphasis on comparative theodicy. Coming from a varied church background, he has been serving at the Summit Evangelical Free Church in Enumclaw, Washington since 2002, where he is currently the teaching pastor. He has also spent significant time working in the technology industry, with most of his time in that industry focused on the area of gaming.

Eric lives in the Pacific Northwest with his wife, Christine, and they recently celebrated their twenty-fifth anniversary. They adopted their son, Ephraim, in 2008. In Eric's spare time, he enjoys travel, reading, theological conversations, and video games. His favorite activity is to connect with friends and discuss life and God.

Bibliography

Adogbo, Michael. Comparative Historical and Interpretive Study of Religions. Lagos Mainland: Malthouse Press Limited, 2010.

Allan, Sarah. "Sons of Suns: Myth and Totemism in Early China," *Bulletin of the School of Oriental and African Studies, University of London*, Vol. 44, No. 2. (1981), 293-301.

Allen, Douglas. "Mircea Eliade's Phenomenological Analysis of Religious Experience," *The Journal of Religion*, Vol. 52, No. 2. (Apr., 1972), 170-186.

Aquinas, St. Thomas. Summa Theologiæ. Translated by Timothy McDermott. Notre Dame, IN: Ave Maria Press, Inc., 1989.

Ariel, David. What Do Jews Believe? The Spiritual Foundations of Judaism. New York, NY: Schocken Books, Inc., 1995.

Avigad, N. "Gleanings from Unpublished Ancient Seals," *Bulletin of the American Schools of Oriental Research*, No. 230, (Apr., 1978), 67-79.

Baldick, Julian. Animal and Shaman: Ancient Religions of Central Asia. New York, NY: I.B. Tauris & Co. Ltd, 2012.

Benson, Elizabeth. "Architecture as Metaphor," *Fifth Palenque Rout Table, 1983*, Vol. 7. (1985).

Birzer, Bradley. J. R. R. Tolkien's Sanctifying Myth: Understanding Middle Earth. Wilmington, DE: Intercollegiate Studies Institute, 2014., Kindle.

Bokser, Baruch. "Approaching Sacred Space," *The Harvard Theological Review*, Vol. 78, No 3/4. (Jul. – Oct., 1985), 279-299.

Bonhoeffer, Dietrich. Creation and Fall, Temptation. New York, NY: Touchstone, 1959.

Bouchard, Constance Brittain. Life and Society in the West. Orlando, FL: Harcourt Brace Jovanovich, Inc., 1988.

Boyd, Carolyn. "Shamanic Journeys into the Otherworld of the Ancient Chichimec," *Latin American Antiquity*, Vol. 7, No. 2. (Jun., 1996), 152-164.

Brady, James. "Settlement Configuration and Cosmology: The Role of Caves at Dos Pilas," *American Anthropologist*, New Series, Vol. 99, No. 3. (Sep., 1997), 602-618.

Braun, Willi and McCutcheon, Russell, Guide to the Study of Religion. New York, NY: T&T Clark, 2000.

Bray, Olive. trans. ed. D. L. Ashliman, *Hávamál: from the Elder or Poetic Edda*, http://pitt.edu/~dash/havamal.html#runes.

Brodeur, Gilchrist. trans. *Gylfaginning: from the Prose Edda*, 1916, http://www.sacred-texts.com/neu/pre/pre04.htm.

Budge, E. *The Legend of Ra and Isis*, Internet Sacred Text Archive, http://www.sacred-texts.com/egy/ebod/ebod07.htm.

___. The Legend of the Gods: The Egyptian Texts. Public Domain. Kindle.

Bukhari, Sahih. *Hadith Collection*, QuranX.com, http://quranx.com/Hadith/Bukhari/USC-MSA/Volume-3/Book-43/Hadith-658/.

Carrasco, David. "City as Symbol in Aztec Thought: The Clues from the Codex Mendoza," *History of Religions*, Vol. 20, No. 3. (Feb., 1981), 199-223.

Cammann, Schuyler. "Religious Symbolism in Persian Art," *History of Religions*, Vol. 15, No. 3. (Feb., 1976), 193-208.

Childs, Craig. "Stonehenges all around us," *Los Angeles Times*, February 16, 2007, http://www.latimes.com/news/opinion/la-oe-childs16feb16,0,5843083.story?coll=la-opinion-center.

Conges, Anne. Glanum. From Salluvian oppidum to Roman city. Éditions du Patrimoine.

Crane, Rachel and Morales, Claudia. "Science and religion fight over Hawaii's highest point," CNN, August 27, 2015, http://www.cnn.com/2015/08/27/us/tmt-hawaii-telescope-controversy/index.html.

Dames, Michael. The Avebury Cycle. London: Thames & Hudson, 1996.

Dante. The Inferno. Translated by John Ciardi. New York, NY: Penguin Group, 1954.

Demetrio, Francisco. "Towards an Understanding of Philippine Myths," *Asian Folklore Studies*, Vol. 37, No. 1. (1978), 25-56.

DeRoche, Michael. "Isaiah XLV 7 and the Creation of Chaos?," *Vetus Testamentum*, Vol. 42, Fasc. 1. (Jan., 1992), 11-21.

Desmangles, Leslie. "African Interpretations of the Christian Cross in Vodun," *Sociological Analysis*, Vol. 38, No. 1. (Spring, 1977), 13-24.

Downing, David. "Sub-Creation or Smuggled Theology: Tolkien contra Lewis on Christian Fantasy," C.S. Lewis Institute, http://www.cslewisinstitute.org/node/1207.

El-Khatib, Abdallah. "Jerusalem in the Quran," *British Journal of Middle Eastern Studies*, Vol. 28, No. 1, (May, 2001), 25-53.

Eldredge, John. Waking the Dead. Nashville, TN: Nelson Books, 2003.

Eliade, Mircea. A History of Religious Ideas Volume 1. Translated by Willard R. Trask. Chicago, IL: University of Chicago Press, 1978.

—. A History of Religious Ideas Volume 2. Translated by Willard R. Trask. Chicago, IL: University of Chicago Press, 1982.

—. "Australian Religions: An Introduction. Part II," *History of Religions*, Vol. 6, No. 3. (Feb., 1967), 208-235.

—. Images and Symbols. Translated by Philip Mairet. Princeton, NJ: Princeton University Press, 1991.

—. Myth and Reality. Translated by Willard R. Trask. Long Grove, IL: Waveland Press, Inc., 1963.

—. Occultism, Witchcraft & Cultural Fashions: Essays in Comparative Religion. Chicago, IL: University of Chicago Press, 1978. Kindle.

—. Patterns in Comparative Religion. Translated by Rosemary Sheed. Lincoln, NE: University of Nebraska Press, 1958.

—. Rites and Symbols of Initiation. Translated by Willard Trask. Putnam, CT: Spring Publications, Inc., 1958.

—. "Some Observations on European Witchcraft," History of Religions, Vol. 14, No. 3. (Feb., 1975), 149-172.

—. The Myth of the Eternal Return. Translated by Willard R. Trask. Princeton, NJ: Princeton University Press, 1954.

__. The Quest: History and Meaning in Religion. Chicago, IL: University of Chicago Press, 1969. Kindle.

—. The Sacred and the Profane. Translated by Willard R. Trask. New York, NY: Harcourt, Inc., 1957.

Erickson, Millard J. Christian Theology. 2nd Edition. Grand Rapids, MI: Baker Academic, 2005.

Faure, B. "Space and Place in Chinese Religious Traditions," History of Religions, Vol. 26, No. 4. (May, 1987), 337-356.

Feder, Kenneth L. and Park, Michael Alan. Human Antiquity. 2nd Edition. Mountain View, CA: Mayfield Publishing Company, 1993.

Feder, Kenneth L. Frauds, Myths, and Mysteries. Mountain View, CA: Mayfield Publishing Company, 1990.

Flom, George. "Sun-Symbols of the Tomb-Sculptures at Loughcrew, Ireland, Illustrated by Similar Figures in Scandinavian Rock-Tracings," American Anthropologist, New Series, Vol. 26, No. 2. (Apr. - Jun., 1924), 139-159.

Forde, Gerhard O. Where God Meets Man. Minneapolis, MN: Augsburg Publishing House, 1972.

Frame, John M. No Other God. Phillipsburg, NJ: P & R Publishing, 2001.

Friedman, Maurice. "Religious Symbolism and 'Universal' Religion," *The Journal of Religion*, Vol. 38, No. 4. (Oct., 1958), 215-225.

Fritz, John and Michell, George. "Interpreting the Plan of a Medieval Hindu Capital, Vijayanagara," *World Archaeology*, Vol. 19, No. 1, (Jun., 1987), 105-129.

Geertz, Armin. "A Reed Pierced the Sky: Hopi Indian Cosmography on the Third Mesa, Arizona," *Numen*, Vol. 31, Fasc. 2. (Dec., 1984), pp. 216-241.

Geisler, Norman and Corduan, Winfried. Philosophy of Religion. Eugene, OR: Wipf and Stock Publishers, 1998.

Geisler, Norman. Systematic Theology Volume 1. Bloomington, MN: Bethany House Publishers, 2002.

Gethin, R. The Foundations of Buddhism. New York, NY: Oxford University Press, 1998.

Grudem, Wayne. Systematic Theology. Grand Rapids, MI: Zondervan, 1994.

Haddad, H. "'Georgic' Cults and Saints of the Levant," *Numen*, Vol. 16, Fasc. 1. (Apr., 1969), pp. 21-39.

Hadley, Judith. The Cult of Asherah in Ancient Israel and Judah: Evidence for a Hebrew Goddess. Cambridge, UK: Cambridge University Press, 2000.

Harms, William. "Ancient Assyrian Rituals Re-enacted for Laying Oriental Institute Cornerstone," The University of Chicago News Office, June 3, 1997, http://www-news.uchicago.edu/releases/97/970603.oriental.cstone.shtml.

Heiser, Michael. The Unseen Realm. Bellingham, WA: Lexham Press, 2015.

Homer. The Iliad. Translated by Richmond Lattimore. Chicago, IL: University of Chicago Press, 1951.

—. The Odyssey of Homer. Translated by Richmond Lattimore. New York, NY: HarperPerennial, 1965.

Hornblower, G. "Kings and Temples of Ancient Egypt," *Man*, Vol. 31, (Apr., 1931), 70-71.

Hosoi, Y. "The Sacred Tree in Japanese Prehistory," *History of Religions*, Vol. 16, No. 2. (Nov., 1976), 95-119.

Ingham, John. "Human Sacrifices at Tenochtitlan," *Comparative Studies in Society and History*, Vol. 26, No. 3. (Jul., 1984), 379-400.

Irwin, John. "The Sacred Anthill and the Cult of the Primordial Mound," *History of Religions*, Vol. 21, No. 4. (May, 1982), 339-360.

Jacobsen, Thorkild. "The Battle between Marduk and Tiamat," *Journal of the American Oriental Society*, Vol. 88, No. 1. (Jan. - Mar., 1968), 104-108.

James, Edwin. The Tree of Life: An Archaeological Study. Leiden, Netherlands: Brill Academic Publishers, 1997.

Janin, H. & Kahlmeyer, A. Islamic Law: The Sharia from Muhammad's Time to the Present. Jefferson, NC: McFarland & Company, Inc. 2007.

Jones, Rex. "Shamanism in South Asia: A Preliminary Survey," *History of Religions*, Vol. 7, No. 4. (May, 1968), 330-347.

Josephus, Flavius. The New Complete Works of Josephus. Translated by William Whiston. Grand Rapids, MI: Kregel Publications, 1999.

Juli. "Seenot." In Love. Comp. Eva Briegel, Andreas Herde, Jonas Pfetzing (music) Eva Briegel (lyrics). 2010.

Keathly, Kenneth. Salvation and Sovereignty: A Molinist Approach. Nashville, TN: B&H Publishing Group, 2010. Kindle.

Kim, Jay. "Hierophany and History," *Journal of the American Academy of Religion*, Vol. 40, No. 3. (Sep., 1972), 334-348.

Knipe, David. "The Heroic Theft: Myths from the Rigveda IV and the Ancient near East," *History of Religions*, Vol. 6, No. 4. (May, 1967), 328-360.

Korom, Frank. "Of Navels and Mountains: A Further Inquiry into the History of an Idea," *Asian Folklore Studies*, Vol. 51, No. 1. (1992), 103-125.

Lavell, Florence. "Biblical and Classical Myths," *The Classical Journal*, Vol. 50, No. 6. (Mar., 1955), 271-278 + 288.

Littleton, C. Scott. Gods, Goddesses, and Mythology. Vol. 11. Tarrytown: Marshall Cavendish Corporation, 2005.

Livius.org, "Mainz, Jupiter Column," *Livius: Culture, geschiedenis en lieteratuur*, April 24, 2106, http://www.livius.org/articles/place/mogontiacum-mainz/mogontiacum-mainz-photos/mainz-jupiter-column/.

Long, Charles. "The West African High God: History and Religious Experience," *History of Religions*, Vol. 3, No. 2. (Winter, 1964), 328-242.

Mabbett, I. "The Symbolism of Mount Meru," *History of Religions*, Vol. 23, No. 1. (Aug., 1983), 64-83.

Maringer, Johannes. "Adorants in Prehistoric Art: Prehistoric Attitudes and Gestures of Prayer," *Numen*, Vol. 26, Fasc. 2. (Dec., 1979), 215-230.

Marschack, Alexander. "Upper Paleolithic Symbol Systems of the Russian Plain: Cognitive and Comparative Analysis [and Comments and Reply]," *Current Anthropology*, Vol. 20, No. 2. (Jun., 1979), 271-311.

May, Herbert. "Pattern and Myth in the Old Testament," *The Journal of Religion*, Vol. 21, No. 3. (Jul., 1941), 285-299.

__. "The Sacred Tree on Palestine Painted Pottery," *Journal of the American Oriental Society*, Vol. 59, No. 2. (Jun., 1939), 251-259.

Meilaender, Gilbert. The Freedom of a Christian. Grand Rapids, MI: Brazos Press, 2006.

Metevelis, Peter. Japanese Mythology and the Primeval World: A Comparative Symbolic Approach. Bloomington, IL: iUniverse, 2009.

Mitchell, Stephen, trans. Bhagavad Gita. New York, NY: Three Rivers Press, 2000.

Moreland, J.P. Scaling the Secular City. Grand Rapids, MI: Baker Book House Company, 1987.

Murison, Ross. "The Serpent in the Old Testament," *The American Journal of Semitic Languages and Literatures*, Vol. 21, No. 2. (Jan., 1905), 115-130.

Muss-Arnolt, W. "The Babylonian Account of Creation," *The Biblical World*, Vol. 3, No. 1. (Jan., 1894), 17-27.

NASB Study Bible. Grand Rapids, MI: Zondervan, 1999.

Neville, David and Matthews, Philip, editors. Faith and Freedom. Hindmarsh, Australia: ATF Press, 2003.

Neumann, Franke. "The Flayed God and His Rattle-Stick: A Shamanic Element in Pre-Hispanic in Mesoamerican Religion," *History of Religions*, Vol. 15, No. 3. (Feb., 1976), 251-263.

Odell-Hein, Eric. "Archaic Water Symbolism and the Determinacy of Evil." Longview, WA: Columbia Evangelical Seminary, 2005. Paper.

Olson, Carl. "Theology of Nostalgia: Reflections on the Theological Aspects of Eliade's Work," *Numen*, Vol. 36, Fasc. 1. (Jun., 1989), 98-112.

Oppenheimer, A. "Analysis of an Assyrian Ritual (Kar 139)," *History of Religions*, Vol. 5, No. 2. (Winter, 1966), 250-265.

Oppenheimer, Clive. Eruptions that Shook the World. New York, NY: Cambridge University Press, 2011.

Otto, Rudolf. The Idea of the Holy. Translated by John W. Harvey. New York, NY: Oxford University Press, 1950.

Paine, Thomas. The Age of Reason Part I. 2nd Edition. New York, NY: Macmillan Publishing Company, 1948.

Parker, Arthur. "Certain Iroquois Tree Myths and Symbols," *American Anthropologist*, New Series, Vol. 14, No. 4. (Oct. – Dec., 1912), 608-620.

Parpola, Simo. "The Assyrian Tree of Life: Tracing the Origins of Jewish Monotheism and Greek Philosophy," *Journal of Near Eastern Studies*, Vol. 52, No. 3. (Jul., 1993), 161-208.

Pinnock, Clark H. Most Moved Mover. Grand Rapids, MI: Baker Academic, 2001.

__. The Openness of God. Downers Grove, IL: InterVarsity Press, 1994.

Piper, John; Taylor, Justin; Helseth, Paul; ed. Beyond the Bounds. Wheaton, IL: Crossway Books, 2003.

Pongratz-Leisten, Beate. "Sacred Marriage and the Transfer of Divine Knowledge: Alliances between the Gods and the King in Ancient Mesopotamia," *Sacred Marriages. The Divine-Human Sexual Metaphor from Sumer to Early Christianity*, Winona Lake, IN: Eisenbrauns, 2008.

Porter, J. "Muhammad's Journey to Heaven," *Numen*, Vol. 21, Fasc. 1. (Apr., 1974), 64-80.

Ray, Benjamin. "Sacred Space and Royal Shrines in Buganda," *History of Religions*, Vol. 16, No. 4, The Mythic Imagination. (May, 1977), 363-373.

Sanders, N.K., trans. The Epic of Gilgamesh. New York, NY: Penguin Books, 1972.

—. The Francis A. Schaeffer Trilogy. Westchester, IL: Crossway Books, 1990.

Sayce, A. "The Babylonian and Biblical Accounts of the Creation," *The American Journal of Theology*, Vol. 9, No. 1. (Jan., 1905), 1-9.

Scranton, Laird. The Cosmological Origins of Myth and Symbol: From the Dogon and Ancient Egypt to India, Tibet, and China. Rochester, VT: Inner Traditions, 2010.

Shriner, Larry. "Sacred Space, Profane Space, Human Space," *Journal of the American Academy of Religion*, Vol. 40, No. 4. (Dec., 1972), 425-436.

Smith, Louise. "Light from North Syria on Old Testament Interpretation," *Journal of Bible and Religion,* Vol. 7, No. 4. (Nov., 1939), 185-190.

Souden, David. Stonehenge. London, United Kingdom: Collins & Brown Ltd, 1997.

Stephens, Ferris. "The Babylonian Dragon Myth in Habakkuk 3," *Journal of Biblical Literature*, Vol. 43, No. 3/4. (1924), p. 290-293.

Thomsen, Elsebeth. "New Light on the Origin on the Holy Black Stone of the Ka'ba," *Meteoritics*, Vol. 15, No. 1, (Mar., 1980).

Tolkien, J.R.R. The Lord of the Rings. New York, NY: Houghton Mifflin Company, 1991.

UCLA James S. Coleman African Studies Center, "Sacred Circles: 2000 Years of North American Indian Art," *African Arts*, Vol. 10, No. 2. (Jan., 1977).

Varner, Gary. The Mythic Forest, the Green Man, and the Spirit of Nature. New York, NY: Algora Publishing, 2006.

Wakeman, Mary. "The Biblical Earth Monster in the Cosmogonic Combat Myth," *Journal of Biblical Literature*, Vol. 88, No. 3. (Sep., 1969), 313-320.

Ward, William. "The Asserted Seven-Fold Division of the Sacred Tree," *Journal of the Society of Biblical Literature and Exegesis*, Vol. 8, No. 1/2. (Jun. - Dec., 1888).

Watanabe, John. "From Saints to Shibboleths: Image, Structure, and Identity in Maya Religious Syncretism," *American Ethnologist*, Vol. 17, No. 1. (Feb., 1990).

Waterman, Leroy. "Cosmogonic Affinities in Genesis 1:2," *The American Journal of Semitic Languages and Literatures*, Vol. 43, No. 3. (Apr., 1927), 177-184.

Whipps, Heather. "Mythic Birthplace of Zeus Said Found," *Live Science*, February 9, 2009, http://www.livescience.com/history/090209-zeus-origin.html.

White, K. "The Sacred Grove: A Comparative Study of Some Parallel Aspects of Religious Ritual in Ancient Crete and the Near East," *Greece & Rome*, 2nd Ser., Vol. 1, No. 3. (Oct., 1954), 112-127.

Wilkins, Robert and Lewis, Rob. The Church of Irresistible Influence. Grand Rapids, MI: Zondervan, 2001.

Winston, King. "Śūnyatā as a Master-Symbol." *Numen* 17, fasc. 2 (Aug., 1970). 95-104.

Wright, N. T. Evil and the Justice of God. Downers Grove, IL: InterVarsity Press, 2006.

Urban, Wilbur. "Symbolism as a Theological Principle." *The Journal of Religion* 19, no. 1 (Jan., 1939).

Yu, David. "The Creation Myth and Its Symbolism in Classical Taoism," *Philosophy East and West*, Vol. 31, No. 4. (Oct., 1981).

Zacharias, Ravi. Jesus Among Other Gods. Nashville, TN: W Publishing Group, 2000.

Notes

1   Mircea Eliade, *Patterns in Comparative Religion* (Lincoln, NE: University of Nebraska Press, 1996), p. 33.

2   Kenneth L. Feder and Michael Alan Park, *Human Antiquity,* 2nd Edition (Mountain View, CA: Mayfield Publishing Company, 1993), pp. 7-11.

3   Mircea Eliade, *Myth and Reality* (Long Grove, IL: Waveland Press, Inc., 1963), pp. 12, 18-19, 92.

4   Norman Geisler, *Systematic Theology,* vol. 1 (Bloomington, MN: Bethany House Publishers, 2002), p. 229.

5   A single standing stone as opposed to a full stone circle.

6   Norman Geisler and Winfried Corduan, *Philosophy of Religion* (Grand Rapids, MI: Baker Books, 90), pp. 16-17.

7   Ibid., pp. 16, 26, 39.

8   Rudolf Otto, *The Idea of the Holy* (New York, NY: Oxford University Press, 1950), p. 9ff.

9   This study also builds from Eliade's academic foundation, particularly his categorization and explanation of the human perception of the

sacred. Much of this work is indebted to Eliade's broad, prolific, and erudite observations, and his work is cited repeatedly throughout.

[10] Millard J. Erickson, *Christian Theology* (Grand Rapids, MI: Baker Academic, 2005), pp 41-42.

[11] Graeme Garrett, "Open Heaven/Closed Hearts," in *Faith and Freedom* (Hindmarsh, Australia: ATF Press, 2003), pp. 73-74.

[12] Wilbur M. Urban, "Symbolism as a Theological Principle," in *The Journal of Religion*, Vol. 19, No. 1. (Jan., 1939), pp. 7-8.

[13] Winston L. King, "Śūnyatā as a Master-Symbol," in *Numen*, Vol. 17, Fasc. 2. (Aug., 1970), p. 96.

[14] Dietrich Bonhoeffer, *Creation and Fall, Temptation* (New York, NY: Touchstone, 1959), p. 53.

[15] John Eldredge, *Waking the Dead* (Nashville, TN: Nelson Books, 2003), p. 26.

[16] Bradley J. Birzer, *J. R. R. Tolkien's Sanctifying Myth: Understanding Middle Earth* (Wilmington, DE: Intercollegiate Studies Institute, 2014), 57-61, Kindle.

[17] Maurice S. Friedman, "Religious Symbolism and 'Universal' Religion," in *The Journal of Religion*, Vol. 38, No. 4. (Oct., 1958), p. 216.

[18] *The American Heritage Dictionary of the English Language*, executive ed. Peter Davies, s.v. "syn-," (Boston, MA: Houghton Mifflin Co, 1981).

[19] Mircea Eliade, *Images and Symbols* (Princeton, NJ: Princeton University Press, 1991), p. 157.

[20] Otto, pp. 3-4.

[21] Catholic Online, *St. George*, in the Catholic Online, accessed May 6, 2017, http://www.catholic.org/saints/saint.php?saint_id=280.

[22] H. S. Haddad, "'Georgic' Cults and Saints of the Levant," in *Numen*, Vol. 16, Fasc. 1. (Apr., 1969), pp. 21-39.

23   John M. Watanabe, "From Saints to Shibboleths: Image, Structure, and Identity in Maya Religious Syncretism," in *American Ethnologist*, Vol. 17, No. 1. (Feb., 1990), pp. 135-139.

24   Richard Horsley, "Further Reflections on Witchcraft and European Folk Religion," in *History of Religions*, Vol. 19, No. 1. (Aug., 1979), pp. 76-84.

25   Mircea Eliade, "Some Observations on European Witchcraft," in *History of Religions*, Vol. 14, No. 3. (Feb., 1975), pp. 153-156.

26   Thomas Paine, *The Age of Reason*, part 1 (New York, NY: Macmillan Publishing Company, 1948), p. 7.

27   Eliade, *Sacred*, p. 27.

28   Ibid., p. 212.

29   Wayne Grudem, *Systematic Theology* (Grand Rapids, MI: Zondervan, 1994), p. 47ff.

30   Ibid., p. 90ff.

31   Armin W. Geertz, "A Reed Pierced the Sky: Hopi Indian Cosmography on the Third Mesa, Arizona," in *Numen*, Vol. 31, Fasc. 2. (Dec., 1984), pp. 216-241.

32   David Carrasco, "City as Symbol in Aztec Thought: The Clues from the Codex Mendoza," in *History of Religions*, Vol. 20, No. 3. (Feb., 1981), pp. 199-223.

33   John M. Ingham, "Human Sacrifices at Tenochtitlan," in *Comparative Studies in Society and History*, Vol. 26, No. 3. (Jul., 1984), pp. 386.

34   Rex L. Jones, "Shamanism in South Asia: A Preliminary Survey," in *History of Religions*, Vol. 7, No. 4. (May, 1968), pp. 333-342.

35   Aeschylus, *Aeschylus I: Oresteia* (Chicago, IL: University of Chicago Press, 1953), p. 97.

36   W. Muss-Arnolt, "The Babylonian Account of Creation," in *The Biblical World*, Vol. 3, No. 1. (Jan., 1894), p. 18.

37 Mary K. Wakeman, "The Biblical Earth Monster in the Cosmogonic Combat Myth," in *Journal of Biblical Literature*, Vol. 88, No. 3. (Sep., 1969), p. 316.

38 Mircea Eliade, *Occultism, Witchcraft, and Cultural Fashions: Essays in Comparative Religion* (Chicago, IL: University of Chicago Press, 1976), 1478-1491, Kindle.

40 Eliade, *Patterns*, pp. 38-39.

41 Geisler and Corduan, p. 35.

42 Eliade, *Patterns*, pp. 38-41.

43 Ibid., p. 38.

44 Johannes Maringer, "Adorants in Prehistoric Art: Prehistoric Attitudes and Gestures of Prayer," in *Numen*, Vol. 26, Fasc. 2. (Dec., 1979), pp. 215-230.

45 George T. Flom, "Sun-Symbols of the Tomb-Sculptures at Loughcrew, Ireland, Illustrated by Similar Figures in Scandinavian Rock-Tracings," in *American Anthropologist*, New Series, Vol. 26, No. 2. (Apr. - Jun., 1924), pp. 139-159.

46 Charles H. Long, "The West African High God: History and Religious Experience," in *History of Religions*, Vol. 3, No. 2. (Winter, 1964), p. 333.

47 Eliade, *Patterns*, p. 40.

48 Y. T. Hosoi, "The Sacred Tree in Japanese Prehistory," in *History of Religions*, Vol. 16, No. 2. (Nov., 1976), pp. 95-119.

49 Eliade, *Patterns*, p. 60.

50 Homer, *The Odyssey of Homer* (New York, NY: HarperPerennial, 1965), p. 88.

51 Eliade, *Patterns*, p. 64.

52 Simo Parpola, "The Assyrian Tree of Life: Tracing the Origins of Jewish Monotheism and Greek Philosophy," in *Journal of Near Eastern Studies*, Vol. 52, No. 3. (Jul., 1993), p. 181.

53 Ibid., pp. 184-185.

54   Ibid., p. 187.

55   N. Avigad, "Gleanings from Unpublished Ancient Seals," in *Bulletin of the American Schools of Oriental Research*, No. 230, (Apr., 1978), p 68.

56   E. A. Wallis Budge, *The Legend of Ra and Isis*, Internet Sacred Text Archive, accessed May 9, 2017, http://www.sacred-texts.com/egy/ebod/ebod07.htm.

57   Schuyler V. R. Cammann, "Religious Symbolism in Persian Art," in *History of Religions*, Vol. 15, No. 3. (Feb., 1976), pp. 193-208.

58   Eliade, *Sacred*, p. 119ff.

59   C. Scott Littleton, *Gods, Goddesses, and Mythology* (Tarrytown, NY: Marshall Cavendish Corporation, 2005), pp. 711-712.

60   Flavius Josephus, *The New Complete Works of Josephus* (Grand Rapids, MI: Kregel Publications, Inc., 1999), p. 126.

61   Carl Olson, "Theology of Nostalgia: Reflections on the Theological Aspects of Eliade's Work," in *Numen*, Vol. 36, Fasc. 1. (Jun., 1989), p. 102.

62   Ibid.

63   Eliades *Images*, p. 40.

64   Mircea Eliade, "Australian Religions: An Introduction. Part II," in *History of Religions*, Vol. 6, No. 3. (Feb., 1967), pp. 212-213.

65   Benjamin Ray, "Sacred Space and Royal Shrines in Buganda," in *History of Religions*, Vol. 16, No. 4, The Mythic Imagination. (May, 1977), pp. 364-366.

66   Feder and Park, p. 4.

67   Florence B. Lavell, "Biblical and Classical Myths," in *The Classical Journal*, Vol. 50, No. 6. (Mar., 1955), pp. 271-272.

68   Eliade, *Sacred*, p. 35.

69   Ibid., p. 11.

70   Ibid.

71 Jay J. Kim, "Hierophany and History," in *Journal of the American Academy of Religion*, Vol. 40, No. 3. (Sep., 1972), p. 334.

72 Juli, "Seenot," *In Love*, Universal Music Domestic Pop, 2010.

73 This happens to be my favorite song, both for its haunting presentation and for its lyrical content, which I am sure I ascribe far more meaning to than was intended by the lyricist.

74 Eliade, *Sacred*, pp. 20-24, 30.

75 Ibid., p. 21.

76 Kim, p. 348.

77 Willi Braun and Russel McCutcheon, *Guide to the Study of Religion* (New York, NY: T&T Clark, 2000), p. 183.

78 Eliade, *Sacred*, p. 121.

79 Ibid., p. 28.

80 Peter Metevelis, *Japanese Mythology and the Primeval World: A Comparative Symbolic Approach* (Bloomington, IL: iUniverse, 2009), pp. 205ff.

81 Elsebeth Thomsen, "New Light on the Origin on the Holy Black Stone of the Ka'ba," in *Meteoritics*, Vol. 15, No. 1, (Mar., 1980), pp. 87-90.

82 Sahih Bukhari, *Hadith Collection*, QuranX.com, accessed May 6, 2017, http://quranx.com/Hadith/Bukhari/USC-MSA/Volume-3/Book-43/Hadith-658/.

83 Michael Adogbo, *Comparative Historical and Interpretive Study of Religions* (Lagos Mainland: Malthouse Press Limited, 2010), p. 4.

84 Douglas Allen, "Mircea Eliade's Phenomenological Analysis of Religious Experience," in *The Journal of Religion*, Vol. 52, No. 2. (Apr., 1972), pp. 179-180.

85 Larry Shriner, "Sacred Space, Profane Space, Human Space," in *Journal of the American Academy of Religion*, Vol. 40, No. 4. (Dec., 1972), p. 426.

86 K. D. White, "The Sacred Grove: A Comparative Study of Some Parallel Aspects of Religious Ritual in Ancient Crete and the Near East," in *Greece & Rome*, 2nd Ser., Vol. 1, No. 3. (Oct., 1954), p. 115.

87 Eliade, *Patterns*, p. 368.

88 Frank J. Korom, "Of Navels and Mountains: A Further Inquiry into the History of an Idea," in *Asian Folklore Studies*, Vol. 51, No. 1. (1992), pp 106-108.

89 Eliade, *Sacred*, pp. 36-37.

90 Carolyn E. Boyd, "Shamanic Journeys into the Otherworld of the Ancient Chichimec," in *Latin American Antiquity*, Vol. 7, No. 2. (Jun., 1996), p. 156.

91 Eliade, *Patterns*, p. 29.

92 Eliade, *Images,* p. 40.

93 Eliade, *Sacred*, pp. 22-23.

94 Ibid.

95 Ibid.

96 Ibid., pp. 37-38.

97 A. Leo Oppenheim, "Analysis of an Assyrian Ritual (Kar 139)," in *History of Religions*, Vol. 5, No. 2. (Winter, 1966), pp. 250-265.

98 Beate Pongratz-Leisten, "Sacred Marriage and the Transfer of Divine Knowledge: Alliances between the Gods and the King in Ancient Mesopotamia," in *Sacred Marriages. The Divine-Human Sexual Metaphor from Sumer to Early Christianity* (Winona Lake, IN: Eisenbrauns, 2008), p. 69.

99 Eliade, *Patterns*, pp. 100-101, 265-326.

100 James E. Brady, "Settlement Configuration and Cosmology: The Role of Caves at Dos Pilas," in *American Anthropologist*, New Series, Vol. 99, No. 3. (Sep., 1997), pp. 603-604.

101 Boyd, p. 157.

[102] John C. Irwin, "The Sacred Anthill and the Cult of the Primordial Mound," in *History of Religions*, Vol. 21, No. 4. (May, 1982), pp. 342-343.

[103] Eliade, *Patterns*, p. 13.

[104] Mircea Eliade, *The Myth of the Eternal Return* (Princeton, NJ: Princeton University Press, 1954), pp. 3-4.

[105] A henge is a circular area, usually surrounded by a bank of earth or a ditch, often containing large, standing pillars of stone or wood. People generally used them for ritual purposes and for marking astronomical events (which were also religious rituals referencing the upper sky realm at their core). Stonehenge is the most recognizable of henges, but there are hundreds all over northern Europe, particularly in the British Isles.

[106] Michael Dames, *The Avebury Cycle* (London: Thames & Hudson, 1996), p. 9.

[107] A megalith is a large stone, either natural or shaped by people, often used as part of a memorial, monument, sacred site, etc.

[108] Otto, p. 66.

[109] Eliade, *Patterns*, p. 232.

[110] Eliade, *Images,* p. 40.

[111] Livius.org, "Mainz, Jupiter Column," *Livius: Culture, geschiedenis en lieteratuur*, April 24, 2106, accessed May 6, 2017, http://www.livius.org/articles/place/mogontiacum-mainz/mogontiacum-mainz-photos/mainz-jupiter-column/.

[112] David Souden, *Stonehenge* (London, United Kingdom: Collins & Brown Ltd., 1997), p. 128.

[113] Craig Childs, "Stonehenges all around us," *Los Angeles Times*, February 16, 2007, accessed October 18, 2007, http://www.latimes.com/news/opinion/la-oe-childs16feb16,0,5843083.story?coll=la-opinion-center.

114 Kenneth L. Feder, *Frauds, Myths, and Mysteries* (Mountain View, CA: Mayfield Publishing Company, 1990), pp. 195-196.

115 Eliade, *Patterns*, p. 216.

116 Ibid. p. 25.

117 Eliade, *Sacred*, p. 22ff.

118 Eliade, *Patterns*, pp. 230-231.

119 Ibid., pp. 99-101.

120 Homer, *The Iliad* (Chicago, IL: University of Chicago Press, 1951), p. 72.

121 Shiner, pp. 432-433.

122 Heather Whipps, "Mythic Birthplace of Zeus Said Found," *Live Science*, February 9, 2009, accessed February 10, 2009, http://www.livescience.com/history/090209-zeus-origin.html.

123 I. W. Mabbett, "The Symbolism of Mount Meru," in *History of Religions*, Vol. 23, No. 1. (Aug., 1983), pp. 64-83.

124 Bernard Faure, "Space and Place in Chinese Religious Traditions," in *History of Religions*, Vol. 26, No. 4. (May, 1987), p. 340.

125 A world-mountain is a mountain along which lies the central spiritual axis of the world, also sometimes the center point of Divine creation, and even sometimes a central point of alignment for the celestial bodies as well.

126 Eliade, *Images*, p. 42.

127 N.K. Sanders, trans., *The Epic of Gilgamesh* (New York, NY: Penguin Books, 1972), p. 70.

128 Eliade, *Images*, p. 42.

129 Michael Heiser, *The Unseen Realm: Recovering the supernatural worldview of the Bible*, (Bellingham, WA: Lexham Press, 2015), Kindle.

130 Louise Pettibone Smith, "Light from North Syria on Old Testament Interpretation," in *Journal of Bible and Religion*, Vol. 7, No. 4. (Nov., 1939), p. 187.

[131] Abdallah El-Khatib, "Jerusalem in the Quran," in *British Journal of Middle Eastern Studies*, Vol. 28, No. 1, (May, 2001), p. 26.

[132] Rachel Crane and Claudia Morales, "Science and religion fight over Hawaii's highest point," CNN, August 27, 2015, accessed August 27, 2015, http://www.cnn.com/2015/08/27/us/tmt-hawaii-telescope-controversy/index.html.

[133] Eliade, *Sacred*, p. 26.

[134] Mabbett, pp. 73-64.

[135] Eliade, *Sacred*, p. 41.

[136] Ibid., pp. 40-41.

[137] Constance Brittain Bouchard, *Life and Society in the West* (Orlando, FL: Harcourt Brace Jovanovich, Inc., 1998), p. 14.

[138] Korom, p. 109.

[139] Josephus, p. 274.

[140] Eliade, *Images*, p. 44.

[141] Eliade, *Patterns*, pp. 267-269.

[142] Herbert Gordon May, "The Sacred Tree on Palestine Painted Pottery," in *Journal of the American Oriental Society*, Vol. 59, No. 2. (Jun., 1939), pp. 251-259.

[143] Eliade, *Patterns*, p. 3.

[144] Ibid.

[145] Stephen Mitchell, trans., *Bhagavad Gita* (New York, NY: Three Rivers Press, 2000), pp. 164-165.

[146] Rupert Gethin, *The Foundations of Buddhism* (New York, NY: Oxford University Press, 1998), p. 15.

[147] Eliade, *Patterns*, p. 276.

[148] Arthur C. Parker, "Certain Iroquois Tree Myths and Symbols," in *American Anthropologist*, New Series, Vol. 14, No. 4. (Oct. – Dec., 1912), pp. 608-620.

[149] Olive Bray, trans., *Hávamál: from the Elder or Poetic Edda*, ed. D. L. Ashliman, accessed May 6, 2017, http://pitt.edu/~dash/havamal.html#runes.

[150] Sarah Allan, "Sons of Suns: Myth and Totemism in Early China," in *Bulletin of the School of Oriental and African Studies, University of London*, Vol. 44, No. 2. (1981), pp. 293-301.

[151] Julian Baldick, *Animal and Shaman: Ancient Religions of Central Asia* (New York, NY: I.B. Tauris & Co. Ltd, 2012), p. 70.

[152] William Hayes Ward, "The Asserted Seven-Fold Division of the Sacred Tree," in *Journal of the Society of Biblical Literature and Exegesis*, Vol. 8, No. 1/2. (Jun. - Dec., 1888), pp. 151-155.

[153] Avidad, pp. 68-69.

[154] Edwin James, *The Tree of Life: An Archaeological Study*, (Leiden, Netherlands: Brill Academic Publishers, 1997), p. 42.

[155] Laird Scranton, *The Cosmological Origins of Myth and Symbol: From the Dogon and Ancient Egypt to India, Tibet, and China* (Rochester, VT: Inner Traditions, 2010), pp. 56-58.

[156] J.R.R. Tolkien, *The Lord of the Rings* (New York, NY: Houghton Mifflin Company, 1991), p. 322.

[157] Ibid., p. 569.

[158] Ibid., p. 491.

[159] Ibid., p. 569.

[160] J. R. Porter, "Muhammad's Journey to Heaven," in *Numen*, Vol. 21, Fasc. 1. (Apr., 1974), p. 71.

[161] Franke J. Neumann, "The Flayed God and His Rattle-Stick: A Shamanic Element in Pre-Hispanic in Mesoamerican Religion," in *History of Religions*, Vol. 15, No. 3. (Feb., 1976), pp. 251-263.

[162] Eliade, *Images*, p. 47.

[163] Eliade, *Rites and Symbols of Initiation* (Putnam, CT: Spring Publications, Inc., 1958), p. 89.

[164] Ibid., p. 33.

[165] Eliade, *Occultism*, 362-267, Kindle.

[166] Rex L. Jones, "Shamanism in South Asia: A Preliminary Survey," in *History of Religions*, Vol. 7, No. 4. (May, 1968), p. 335.

[167] Gary Varner, *The Mythic Forest, the Green Man, and the Spirit of Nature*, (New York, NY: Algora Publishing, 2006), p. 114.

[168] Judith Hadley, *The Cult of Asherah in Ancient Israel and Judah: Evidence for a Hebrew Goddess*, (Cambridge, UK: Cambridge University Press, 2000), pp. 2-4.

[169] "Asherah," from JewishEncyclopedia.com, http://www.jewishency-clopedia.com/articles/1942-asherah. Date of access: March 5, 2014.

[170] The subjugation of an ocean or sea is one of the greatest and most universal displays of absolute divinity to ancient people of all cultures and religions.

[171] Anne Congés, *Glanum. From Salluvian oppidum to Roman city*, (Éditions du Patrimoine), pp. 56-69.

[172] Feder and Park, p. 7.

[173] Eliade, *Myth and Reality*, pp. 12, 92.

[174] Mircea Eliade, *A History of Religious Ideas, vol. 1, From the Stone Age to the Eleusinian Mysteries*, (Chicago, IL: University of Chicago Press, 1978), pp. 88-92.

[175] David C. Yu, "The Creation Myth and Its Symbolism in Classical Taoism," in *Philosophy East and West*, Vol. 31, No. 4. (Oct., 1981), pp. 479-480.

[176] Thorkild Jacobsen, "The Battle between Marduk and Tiamat," in *Journal of the American Oriental Society*, Vol. 88, No. 1. (Jan. - Mar., 1968), pp. 104-108.

[177] Herbert Gordon May, "Pattern and Myth in the Old Testament," in *The Journal of Religion*, Vol. 21, No. 3. (Jul., 1941), p. 286.

[178] Francisco R. Demetrio, "Towards an Understanding of Philippine Myths," in *Asian Folklore Studies*, Vol. 37, No. 1. (1978), p. 46.

[179] Eliade, *History vol. 1*, p. 87-88.

180 Ibid.

181 *Utterance 600*, in the Pyramid Texts, accessed May 6, 2017, http://
www.pyramidtexts.com/utterance600.htm.

182 Irwin, pp. 343-345.

183 Eric Odell-Hein. "Archaic Water Symbolism and the Determinacy
of Evil." (Longview, WA: Columbia Evangelical Seminary, 2005).

184 May, *Pattern*, p. 286.

185 Ferris J. Stephens, "The Babylonian Dragon Myth in Habakkuk 3,"
in *Journal of Biblical Literature*, Vol. 43, No. 3/4. (1924), p. 290-293.

186 Eliade, *History vol. 1*, p. 154.?

187 Mircea Eliade, *A History of Religious Ideas, vol. 2, From Gautama
Buddha to the Triumph of Christianity*, (Chicago, IL: University of
Chicago Press, 1982), p. 15.

188 Arthur Gilchrist Brodeur, trans., *Gylfaginning: from the Prose Edda*,
1916, accessed May 6, 2017, http://www.sacred-texts.com/neu/pre/
pre04.htm.

189 A. H. Sayce, "The Babylonian and Biblical Accounts of the
Creation," in *The American Journal of Theology*, Vol. 9, No. 1. (Jan.,
1905), p. 2.

190 May, *Pattern*, p. 286.

191 David M. Knipe, "The Heroic Theft: Myths from the Rigveda IV
and the Ancient near East," in *History of Religions*, Vol. 6, No. 4.
(May, 1967), p. 337.

192 Ross G. Murison, "The Serpent in the Old Testament," in *The
American Journal of Semitic Languages and Literatures*, Vol. 21, No.
2. (Jan., 1905), p. 120.

193 E. A. Wallis Budge, *Legends of the Gods: The Egyptian Texts*, (Public
Domain, 1911), 349-350, Kindle.

194 Clive Oppenheimer, *Eruptions that Shook the World*, (New York,
NY: Cambridge University Press, 2011), pp. 123-124.

[195] E. A. Wallis Budge, *The Babylonian Legends of the Creation*, (Public Domain, 1921), 128-129, Kindle.

[196] Michael Deroche, "Isaiah XLV 7 and the Creation of Chaos?," in *Vetus Testamentum*, Vol. 42, Fasc. 1. (Jan., 1992), pp. 11-12.

[197] Leroy Waterman, "Cosmogonic Affinities in Genesis 1:2," in *The American Journal of Semitic Languages and Literatures*, Vol. 43, No. 3. (Apr., 1927), p.180.

[198] Eliade, *Rites*, 257-258, Kindle.

[199] Eliade, *Patterns*, p. 406.

[200] Eliade, *Sacred*, p. 45.

[201] Ibid., p. 202.

[202] Eliade, *Patterns*, p. 194.

[203] Ibid., pp. 188-195

[204] Some Christian traditions sprinkle infants as opposed to submerging the individual at an older age. The baptisms described in the Bible were full immersion, and that is what this is referencing. In this work I am not taking a theological stance on immersion versus sprinkling. Recognize that even if the method used is sprinkling, it still follows the same symbolic pattern as immersion. Personally, I was baptized in the Evangelische Kirche (Lutheran), in Ludwigsburg, Germany when I was an infant. Later in my life, I decided to be baptized again (immersion) as an intentional believer and dedicated follower of Christ as I approached my teenage years.

[205] Eliade, *Sacred*, p. 20.

[206] UCLA James S. Coleman African Studies Center, "Sacred Circles: 2000 Years of North American Indian Art," in *African Arts*, Vol. 10, No. 2. (Jan., 1977), p. 78.

[207] Eliade, *Rites*, 396-98, Kindle.

[208] Leslie Gerald Desmangles, "African Interpretations of the Christian Cross in Vodun," in *Sociological Analysis*, Vol. 38, No. 1. (Spring, 1977), pp. 13-24.

[209] Mircea Eliade, *The Quest: History and Meaning in Religion*, (Chicago, IL: University of Chicago Press, 1969), 2424-2429, Kindle.

[210] Alexander Marschack, "Upper Paleolithic Symbol Systems of the Russian Plain: Cognitive and Comparative Analysis [and Comments and Reply]," in *Current Anthropology*, Vol. 20, No. 2. (Jun., 1979), pp. 297-298.

[211] G. D. Hornblower, "Kings and Temples of Ancient Egypt," in *Man*, Vol. 31, (Apr., 1931), p. 70.

[212] Eliade, *Images*, p. 32.

[213] David Downing, "Sub-Creation or Smuggled Theology: Tolkien contra Lewis on Christian Fantasy," C.S. Lewis Institute, http://www.cslewisinstitute.org/node/1207, accessed May 2, 2017.

[214] Baruch Bokser, "Approaching Sacred Space," in *The Harvard Theological Review*, Vol. 78, No 3/4. (Jul. – Oct., 1985), pp. 289-290.

[215] William Harms, "Ancient Assyrian Rituals Re-enacted for Laying Oriental Institute Cornerstone," The University of Chicago News Office, June 3, 1997, accessed May 6, 2017, http://www-news.uchicago.edu/releases/97/970603.oriental.cstone.shtml.

[216] Eliade, *Sacred*, p. 54.

[217] Ibid., p. 46.

[218] Ibid.

[219] John M. Fritz and George Michell, "Interpreting the Plan of a Medieval Hindu Capital, Vijayanagara," in *World Archaeology*, Vol. 19, No. 1, (Jun., 1987), pp. 123-124.

[220] Elizabeth P. Benson, "Architecture as Metaphor," in *Fifth Palenque Rout Table, 1983*, Vol. 7. (1985), p. 199.

[221] Eliade, *Sacred*, p. 28.

[222] Ibid.

[223] I hold to the standard orthodox position of plenary, verbal inspiration.

[224] Eliade, *Myth and Reality*, p. 164.

225   Eliade, *Images*, p. 161.

226   Eliade, *Patterns*, p. 230.

227   Ibid., p. 231.

228   J.P. Moreland, *Scaling the Secular City* (Grand Rapids, MI: Baker Book House Company, 1987), p. 128.

229   Clark H. Pinnock, *The Openness of God* (Downers Grove, IL: InterVarsity Press, 1994), pp. 101-102.

230   Christopher D. Marshall, "The Moral Vision of the Beatitudes," in *Faith*, p. 16.

231   Saint Thomas Aquinas, *Summa Theologiæ* (Notre Dame, IN: Ave Maria Press, Inc., 1989), p. 351.

232   Eliade, *Images*, p. 163.

233   Bonhoeffer, *Creation*, p. 107.

234   Eliade, *Patterns*, p. 33.

235   Eliade, *History*, vol. 1, p. 166.

236   Heiser, *The Unseen Realm*. Most of the credit for this goes to Dr. Michael Heiser who laid out a terrific argument for this position over the course of many chapters in his book. This was not the primary thrust of the book, but this position becomes apparent as the whole book is read and considered in the context of the ancient people.

237   Bonhoeffer, pp. 55-56.

238   Eliade, *History*, vol. 1, p. 166.

239   Gilbert Meilaender, *The Freedom of a Christian* (Grand Rapids, MI: Brazos Press, 2006), p. 62.

240   Hunt Janin & Andre Kahlmeyer, *Islamic Law: The Sharia from Muhammad's Time to the Present*, (Jefferson, NC: McFarland & Company, Inc: 2007).

241   David Ariel, *What Do Jews Believe? The Spiritual Foundations of Judaism* (New York, NY: Schocken Books, Inc., 1995), p. 162.

242   Francis A. Schaeffer, *The Francis A. Schaeffer Trilogy* (Westchester, IL: Crossway Books, 1990), p. 171.

243 Gerhard O. Forde, *Where God Meets Man* (Minneapolis, MN: Augsburg Publishing House, 1972), p. 36.

244 Rick Strelan, "The Boundaries of Freedom," in *Faith and Freedom* (Hindmarsh, Australia: ATF Press, 2003), p. 56.

245 *The American Heritage Dictionary of the English Language*, executive ed. Executive ed. Peter Davies, s.v. "freedom," (Boston, MA: Houghton Mifflin Co, 1981).

246 Kenneth Keathly, *Salvation and Sovereignty: A Molinist Approach* (Nashville, TN: B&H Publishing Group, 2010), 1680, Kindle.

247 Strelan, "The Boundaries of Freedom," in *Faith and Freedom*, p. 56.

248 Bonhoeffer, p. 112.

249 Mark R. Talbot, "True Freedom: The Liberty that Scripture Portrays as Worth Having," in *Beyond the Bounds* (Wheaton, IL: Crossway Books, 2003), p. 105.

250 John M. Frame, *No Other God* (Phillipsburg, NJ: P & R Publishing, 2001), p. 131.

251 Maurice S. Friedman, "Religious Symbolism and 'Universal' Religion," in *The Journal of Religion*, Vol. 38, No. 4, (Oct., 1958), p. 225.

252 Ian Barns, "Toward an Australian Post-Constantinian Public Theology," in *Faith and Freedom* (Hindmarsh, Australia: ATF Press, 2003), p. 91.

253 Garrett, p. 64.

254 N. T. Wright, *Evil and the Justice of God* (Downers Grove, IL: InterVarsity Press, 2006), p. 161.

255 Bill Loader, "Christian Communities in Earliest Christianity: The Church before Churches," in *Faith and Freedom* (Hindmarsh, Australia: ATF Press, 2003), p. 45.

256 Eliade, *History*, vol. 2, p. 413.

257 Thorwald Lorenzen, "Jesus Christ and Spirituality," in *Faith and Freedom* (Hindmarsh, Australia: ATF Press, 2003), p. 94.

Order Information

To order additional copies of this book, please visit
www.redemption-press.com.
Also available on Amazon.com and BarnesandNoble.com
Or by calling toll free 1-844-2REDEEM.

CPSIA information can be obtained
at www.ICGtesting.com
Printed in the USA
FFOW04n1941211117
43682545-42528FF